The Tortoise Guide

Starting *and* Building
a Private Practice ...
at Your Own Pace

THE Tortoise GUIDE

Starting *and* Building
a Private Practice ...
at Your Own Pace

Sharon Good

Good Life Press

New York

© 2023 Sharon Good
All rights reserved in all media. This book, or parts thereof, may not be reproduced in any form without the express written permission of the author.

Published by:
Good Life Press
A division of Good Life Coaching Inc.
New York, NY

www.goodlifepress.com
www.goodlifecoaching.com

Disclaimer: The information in this book is offered as a guideline based on the author's experience and is not meant to substitute for professional guidance. For all business decisions, it is strongly advised that you consult with the appropriate professional, such as an accountant or lawyer.

Publisher's Cataloging-in-Publication Data
Names: Good, Sharon, 1950- .
Title: The tortoise guide : starting and building a private practice ... at your own pace / Sharon Good.
Description: New York, NY : Good Life Press, 2023. | Illustrated. | Summary: A step-by-step guide for new entrepreneurs on how to start and run a private practice, whether it be as a life coach, bookkeeper, massage therapist, graphic designer, or any other solo business. Provides a simple guide for those intimidated by the process or slow movers ("tortoises").
Identifiers: LCCN 2023921212 | ISBN 9780982317280 (pbk) | ISBN 9780982317297 (ebook)
Subjects: LCSH: New business enterprises. | Business planning. | Entrepreneurship. | Self-employed. | BISAC: BUSINESS & ECONOMICS / New Business Enterprises. | BUSINESS & ECONOMICS / Entrepreneurship. | BUSINESS & ECONOMICS / Freelance & Self-Employment.
Classification: LCC HD62.5.G66 2023 | DDC 658.1/1 G--dc23
LC record available at https://lccn.loc.gov/2023921212

ISBN 978-0-9823172-8-0 (paperback)
ISBN 978-0-9823172-9-7 (ebook)

Contents

Introduction 1
- So, You Want to Be an Entrepreneur! 1
- Who This Guide Is For 2
- How to Use This Book 4

SECTION I: SETTING THE FOUNDATION 5

Chapter 1: Concerns About Starting a Business 6
- What Does It Take to Start a Professional Practice? 6
- What Type of Business Should I Start? 8
- The Tortoise Factor 9

Chapter 2: Making the Leap from Salaried to Self-Employed 11
- Are You a Planner or a Leaper? 11
- The Differences Between Employment and Self-Employment ... 11
- Addressing the Challenges 12
  - Worksheet: Addressing the Challenges 17
- Managing the Transition 19

Chapter 3: Creating a Vision and Brand for Your Business 22
- Designing a Business to Support Your Needs and Desires 23
  - Purpose or Mission 23
    - Worksheet: Mission Statement 24
  - Services and Products 25
    - Worksheet: Services and Products 26
  - Your Target Audience 27
    - Worksheet: My Ideal Clients 28
  - Marketability 29
  - Pricing Your Services and Products 29
    - Worksheet: Pricing Plan for My Business 32
  - Your Work Schedule 33
    - Worksheet: My Work Schedule 34

- Personnel 35
  - Worksheet: People I Need to Support My Business 36
- Your Vision and Goals 37
  - Worksheet: Dream Big! 38
  - Worksheet: My Vision Statement 41
  - Worksheet: Goals for My Business 42
- Defining Your Brand 43
  - Worksheet: What Makes Me and My Business Unique? 44
- Elevator Speech 47
  - Worksheet: My Elevator Speech 48

SECTION II: LAUNCHING YOUR BUSINESS 49

Chapter 4: The Nuts and Bolts of Business Start-Up 50
- Compliance, Ethics, Licensing, Certification and Insurance Panels 50
- Choosing a Business Name and Professional Title 51
  - Worksheet: My Business Name and Professional Title 53
- Setting Up Your Business Structure and Taxes 54
- Writing a Basic Business Plan 55
- Operations 56
  - Office or Work Space 56
  - Client and Promotional Materials 57
  - Recordkeeping and Taxes 57
  - Getting Help 58
  - Insurance 59
  - Bank Account 59
  - Accepting Payments 60
- Financial Plan 60
  - Worksheet: Business Plan Checklist 62
  - Worksheet: Financial Projections 64
- Transition Plan 65
- Time Management 67
  - Worksheet: My Transition/Time Management Plan 68

Chapter 5: Marketing Your New Business   69
    ◊ Marketing by Doing What You Love   69
    ◊ Setting the Foundation: Website and Social Media   70
    ◊ Other Ways to Market   71

SECTION III: OPERATING YOUR BUSINESS   73
    ◊ The Daily "Grind" and Work/Life Balance   73
    ◊ Serving Your Customers/Managing Products and Services   73
    ◊ Managing Finances   75
    ◊ And More Marketing   77

SECTION IV: PULLING IT ALL TOGETHER   79
    ◊ Determination and Commitment   79
    ◊ Get Support   79
    ◊ Stay Focused and Motivated   80
    ◊ The Tortoise Way: Patience and Persistence   81

RESOURCES   82

About the Author   84

Whatever you can do or dream you can, begin it.
Boldness has genius, power, and magic in it.
~ Johann Wolfgang von Goethe

Introduction

So, You Want to Be an Entrepreneur!

There's nothing like being your own boss! Or so people imagine. They crave the flexibility, creative freedom and income potential that comes with having your own business. But there's a distance between dream and reality, and it's good to go into it with your eyes open.

As a Life, Career, Retirement and Creativity Coach, I come across many people who would love to have their own business and do something that's meaningful to them, but are intimidated by the prospect of starting and running their own enterprise. As a "Tortoise," it feels daunting to have the responsibility of creating a business, drumming up customers and perhaps managing staff.

> "I define a Tortoise as someone with lots of ideas and ambition, but limited energy, time or other resources. You may become easily frustrated or discouraged when the ideas, opportunities and projects come along faster than you can handle them. Like the Tortoise in the fable, we human Tortoises need to go slowly and take a step at a time. It's important for us to have strategies to help us make the most of our time and energy."
> ~ Sharon Good, *The Tortoise Workbook: Strategies for Getting Ahead at Your Own Pace*

If you had told me when I was 20 that I would have my own businesses and even write a book about marketing, I would have laughed hysterically. At that time, I was a theatre major minoring in music, and the business department could have been located on another planet, for all I knew.

I never had any interest in pursuing business, but it seemed to pursue me. My first foray into entrepreneurship was co-founding a small book publishing company with a friend. It was incredibly challenging. I was good at handling the day-to-day functions, as well as the creative aspects, but being responsible for an entity greater than myself scared the heck out of me, and I didn't like it much. Even so, the work we did was exhilarating and fulfilling, and I wouldn't trade that experience for the world.

When I began life coaching, I started a private practice. It was clear to me that I wanted to keep my business small. I had no interest in running a conglomerate with multiple divisions and employees or contractors to manage. I wanted to focus on doing what I love — coaching, teaching and writing — rather than the nuts and bolts of running a business.

What I have learned, though, is that you don't have to be a buttoned-up business person to be a successful entrepreneur. If doing what you love means starting a business and you're committed to staying the course, I can tell you from personal experience that it's doable. You just have to set it up in a way that serves you and your business idea and gives you the lifestyle you want.

So, you don't need a business degree to start a business. What you do need is:

- A viable product or service that you love, or that you can at least get behind enthusiastically
- A workable plan or vision
- A financial plan or strategy
- A way to get business
- Enthusiasm and passion
- Persistence, determination and commitment

All of these are important – and we'll address each of these in this book – but I attribute my success to my determination. There are times when I felt discouraged, but my determination kept me going until success "kicked in." Building a business can take time, and you need to stick with it and not jump ship the first time you hit an obstacle.

> "Nothing in the world can take the place of persistence."
> ~ Calvin Coolidge

Who This Guide Is For

This book is geared toward anyone who wants to set up a professional practice, including, but not limited to:

Personal Services

- Life Coaches
- Image Consultants
- Aestheticians and Cosmetologists
- Hairdressers

- Professional Organizers
- Fitness Trainers
- Yoga, Pilates and Exercise Instructors

Medical and Healing Practitioners
- Psychotherapists and Counselors
- Chiropractors
- Acupuncturists
- Massage Therapists
- Hypnotherapists
- Nutritionists
- Energy Healers
- Reiki Practitioners

Business Professionals
- Executive Coaches and Trainers
- Virtual Assistants
- Bookkeepers
- Accountants
- Graphic and Web Designers
- Consultants
- Freelance Writers and Editors
- Event and Party Planners
- Advertising and Public Relations Consultants
- Interior Designers and Home Stagers
- Marketing Consultants
- Computer Consultants
- Photographers and Videographers
- Florists and Gift Basket Designers
- Financial Planners

… and more!

How to Use This Book

In this book, I've attempted to lay out the various aspects of starting and running a professional practice. Read it through to get the full picture, then use it as a reference to refresh your memory on specific steps.

In Tortoise style, the information is presented simply and clearly, as an overview of the entrepreneurial process, from the perspective of a life coaching instructor (me!) who has taught numerous students how to start their coaching practice. When it comes to the specifics, be sure to consult with an accountant, lawyer and other relevant professionals to set up and run your business properly.

So, dig in! I hope this book inspires you to start a business that brings you tremendous fulfillment, a great lifestyle and professional success!

Section 1: Setting the Foundation

Before building a house, it's always good to have a solid foundation. In this section, we'll create that foundation for your business.

Chapter 1: Concerns About Starting a Business

If this is your first stab at entrepreneurialism, you probably have some concerns and apprehensions. But fear not: Many professionals have successfully navigated the path toward self-employment. All that's required is a willingness to take on the requirements and challenges of launching and running your business and taking the necessary steps.

Personally, I hate when things are complicated. I like any path to be clear and straightforward. And that's how I will present the steps to establishing your professional practice: in a clear, user-friendly way. If you're a fellow Tortoise, so much the better … we'll take it a step at a time. No rush.

What Does It Take to Start a Professional Practice?

Very often, people ask about what it takes to have a successful practice. Certainly, business know-how will come in handy, but you can learn that or hire people who have the necessary skills and knowledge. We'll talk more about that in the coming pages.

But what about you? What qualities do you need in order to succeed with your professional practice?

◆ Passion

Any endeavor, even one you love, has its ups and downs. It's your passion that will get you through the bumpy parts and keep you going when things look bleak. If "passion" is too strong a word, at least find something that's meaningful to you that you can get behind. If it's not something you care about and enjoy, it will be difficult to sustain the energy and momentum you need to succeed. You may not love every minute of working your business, but it's sure nice if you enjoy it most of the time and it gives you a sense of purpose and a good income.

◆ A Marketable Skill or Product

Even if you love what you do, if you want to have a profitable business, other people need to want your product or service enough to part with their money. You may start a business around a skill you already have or get trained in something you'd love to do. You may also develop a unique product, service or technique that people will want.

◆ Persistence, Discipline and Commitment

As the head of a company – especially if you're the whole company – there's no one standing over you to get things done. You have to motivate yourself to do what needs to get done to make your business successful, even when it's scary or overwhelming. The good news is, discipline is a "muscle" that you can build. The more you practice it, the easier it gets.

A companion of discipline is self-motivation, with its higher octave, inspiration. If you have an inner drive – if you love what you do and making things happen – great! If not, don't despair. If you come into this endeavor with a passion, hopefully your commitment won't be far behind.

> "Powerful words come with powerful intent. Where you have passion, strength, courage, and determination, you can accomplish anything!"
>
> ~ K.L. Toth

◆ Support

None of us can do it alone. Even if you are self-motivated, there are many moving parts to managing a professional practice. You can get the help you need to stay on track and manage yourself, as well as the many tasks that come with the territory. This may come in the form of complementary professionals (accountants, bookkeepers, designers, editors, assistants, etc.) or professional support groups. As a life coach, I, of course, have seen the value in having an accountability partner who helps you work out what you need to do, move through any fears or other obstacles, lay out action steps and stay accountable so that you follow through.

If needed, you can always seek support from professional colleagues who are in the same boat and would love to exchange support and ideas with you.

◆ Vision

When you start your business, there will be many naysayers out there, either in your own circle of friends and family or by way of media and discouraging statistics.

Your business is your unique expression. You need to have your own vision, which will work hand-in-hand with your passion. When you have an authentic vision, you have a "lighthouse beacon" to remind you of your purpose for your business when the going gets tough. It will help you differentiate yourself from your competition and stand out in the marketplace; it will give focus and direction to the actions you take to start and run your business; and it will help you reconnect to your purpose when you feel discouraged.

◆ **Patience and Persistence**

Building a business can take time. Be patient, and don't give up. If you have a solid plan, a deep passion for your work, a financial cushion, and an iron will (some call it stubbornness), you can accomplish anything.

One caution: **Don't start a business to escape a job you hate or to avoid the job hunting process.** If you're not prepared to take on the responsibilities, including getting business, it will only backfire in the end.

What Type of Business Should I Start?

You may come to this book with an idea about what your business will be. If not, here are some ideas:

◆ **Consulting**

Many people take a skill set they've used in the business world and become independent consultants or contractors. The advantage is that your credibility is already established, and you most likely have contacts who will want your services. It's not unusual for someone's first client to be their former employer.

◆ **Using Your Skills**

Similarly, you can leverage your skills to work independently. These may be technology skills, a creative skill or craft, a skill such as organizing, a trade such as woodworking or landscaping, and many others.

- ◆ **Franchising**

You can piggyback on a successful brand by purchasing a franchise. A franchise can cost as little as $2,000 and much more. Entrepreneur.com has some great resources for finding franchise opportunities.

- ◆ **Finding a Need and Filling It**

An enterprising entrepreneur will keep an eye on the marketplace and see what's needed. For example, there came a turning point where every business needed a website. This was an opportunity for website designers, as well as do-it-yourself web hosting services. With the popularity of coaching as a profession, numerous support services (especially around marketing and practice-building) have sprung up. One of my clients noticed the popularity of microgreens at farmers' markets and was able to set up a growing station in a spare room with very little capital outlay.

- ◆ **Inventing a Product or Service**

People have amazing ideas – ever watched *Shark Tank*? If you've got one, develop it, make it unique and learn how to file a patent or copyright and bring it to the marketplace. Big ideas may require investors, but there are lots of things that you can do on your own, such as selling your handicrafts on Etsy or eBay.

- ◆ **Pursuing a Passion or Calling**

Is there a dream you relegated to the back burner because it didn't seem possible? Maybe it is! Maybe you feel called to be an artist, write books and do motivational speaking, follow a spiritual calling or work with a cause like animal welfare. If this feels too big, or the timing is not right, scale it down and see what you can do now, then develop it on your own timeline. Start by working for someone else to learn the ropes and, if it's meant to grow into a full-time or part-time business, it will, with your determination and persistence.

The Tortoise Factor

As a trainer of life coaches, my job includes teaching my students how to start and market their coaching practice. Many new practitioners are used to having a job with a steady paycheck, and letting go of that can be scary.

My students come in various ages and life stages, from 20s to "seasoned citizens" in their 80s. Starting a new business does take time, energy and focus. Add to that the Tortoise Factor – where your energy and time may be at a premium. Many people start a new business while working full-time or raising a family, or at an age where they don't have the same level of energy they used to. As a Tortoise, this can be a challenge.

It's important to set realistic goals, pace yourself, and get the help and support you need. Depending on the type and scope of your business, it can take an average of two years for a business to launch and become profitable. Make sure that you do the foundational work to establish your business on solid ground and minimize the risk. Take whatever time you need. Then, keep taking small steps on a regular basis to continue making your business successful.

For more Tortoise self-management strategies and lots of worksheets, check out my book, *The Tortoise Workbook: Strategies for Getting Ahead at Your Own Pace.*

http://www.goodlifepress.com/Tortoise.html

Chapter 2: Making the Leap from Salaried to Self-Employed

If you've been a salaried employee for a long time – maybe all of your adult life – making the mental, emotional and financial transition to being self-employed can be a challenge. But it's still doable. Knowing yourself and preparing for the transition can help you avoid the pitfalls and even have fun starting your practice.

Are You a Planner or a Leaper?

Each of us has a different style for starting something new. We have different levels of "risk tolerance." Some people like to go to school, get training and perhaps a certificate or degree before they move into a new endeavor. My style, which may be yours, is to jump into the deep end and learn to "swim" along the way.

Either way, it's going to take an investment of time, energy and money. It's important to be aware of what you're getting into before you begin. This chapter will help you to vision and plan, so that you can begin your new practice with your eyes open and well-prepared.

In the following sections, you'll create a vision and a transition plan to help you move into your new business, while minimizing the risk.

The Differences Between Employment and Self-Employment

Being an entrepreneur is very different from being a salaried employee. Yes, you have a lot more freedom in choosing your destiny, not to mention your day-to-day activities. But ultimately you, and only you, are responsible for the success of your business, and there are changes that take some getting used to.

For one thing, the **steady paycheck** goes away. Instead, you need to adjust to having "receivables" and budgeting over the ebbs and flows of a variable income. It may be tempting to splurge when a chunk of money comes in, but you need to be prepared for the times when income goes down to a dribble for a month or more.

As you're transitioning into your business, it's wise to have a **financial cushion** that you can fall back on. There may be a period where you have to quit your "day job" in order to have the time you need to devote to developing your business, but you're not yet making enough to cover your bills. Having that cushion will give you the freedom to work on your new business full-time and still pay your bills.

You also need to get used to creating your own **structure and motivation**. It's easy to respond to imposed deadlines from others, but when it's up to you to make the schedule, you may not take the deadlines seriously, if you even have any. In the start-up phase especially, there may not be a schedule where you need to show up for other people, but you still need to get things done to move the business forward. I find there are two common pitfalls when it comes to creating structure:

- Out of enthusiasm or fear, you work on the business 24/7 and your life goes out of balance, often having repercussions on your well-being or your relationships
- You spend half the day having a leisurely brunch, reading the newspaper, dealing with trivia and maybe get in a couple of hours of work, if any

As you transition to self-employment, you may want to work with a coach or other accountability partner to help you map out a schedule and stick to it. If you're working full-time as you begin building your business, you'll need to be realistic about how much time and energy you can give to it, block out time in your calendar and then be rigorous about sticking to your schedule.

In the next chapter, we'll look at creating a vision and plan for your business that will guide and inspire you as you go through the steps of start-up.

Addressing the Challenges

Starting your own business can be extremely exciting. But the excitement is usually accompanied by some fears or apprehension. People feel anxious about starting a business or professional practice for a number of reasons:

- They're afraid to let go of their steady paycheck
- They're afraid they won't be able to replace the income they get from their job
- They lack business skills
- They feel uncomfortable selling themselves or don't want to be "salesy"
- They're afraid they won't be able to get clients and will, therefore, fail
- They don't know how to get clients
- They're uncomfortable or afraid of approaching potential clients and facing rejection
- As a new practitioner, they may be experiencing "imposter syndrome" – the fear that clients will figure out that they really can't do this and, therefore, shouldn't get paid for it, or at least not paid well
- As a Tortoise, they're afraid they won't have the energy to follow through

The good news is, all of these issues can be addressed and shifted. Here are some ideas:

- **Finances** — Build up savings and/or keep your job, so that you have enough capital to keep you going until your business is profitable. At some point, you may want to go part-time to keep an income stream, while allowing yourself more time to develop your new business. In some cases, you'll need to take a loan to finance the start-up costs of your business. Be sure to include the loan payments in your budget (see page 64).

  Get used to not having a steady paycheck. This is a mental shift as well as a practical one. Do what you need to do to have a sense of financial security. Learn to manage inconsistent receivables. In profitable months, be sure to put money aside to cover the slower months. Treat yourself once in awhile, but don't go overboard and put your business (and your livelihood) at risk.

- **Fear** – This is a given. You're doing something new and unpredictable, and it's scary. Face it; feel the fear and do it anyway. Don't run from the fear. Get help if you need it.

  One entrepreneur bought a successful business where he was previously employed. He splurged on things for himself and shoved the bills into a drawer. He showed up at his store one day to find it was locked by the sheriff for non-payment of taxes. The business failed, and he still had to repay the loans he had taken. Don't do that.

- **Creating a new identity** – You're no longer an employee. You're the boss now. If you have employees, you'll need to get used to being the boss and no longer one of the gang.

- **Responsibility** – You're it. If something is going wrong, you're the one who needs to handle it – either by yourself or by getting help.

- **Wearing multiple hats** – As an entrepreneur, you'll manage a variety of tasks: doing the work of the business, marketing, sales, bookkeeping, customer service, etc. Figure out what you can do well and where it's more cost-effective and time-saving to hire someone. If you're stressed with managing the business, you won't have the energy to offer quality work to your clients.

- **Creating your own structure and being accountable** — It's up to you to set the agenda and make sure that the work gets done and that you meet deadlines. Create a work schedule and put it in your calendar. Making commitments to others can help keep you accountable by creating real deadlines, but it's up to you to make sure you can keep those commitments. If you don't, it'll fall on you and jeopardize the success of your business.

- **Discipline/work ethic** – As an entrepreneur, nobody will be standing over you making sure things get done. It will be tempting to shirk work and have lazy days – and you certainly do want to maintain balance in your life – but it's up to you to develop the discipline needed to do what you need to do to get the work done and make the business profitable.

- **Balancing business with personal** — I've found that it helps to have clear boundaries around work vs. personal time. You might stick to the traditional 9 – 5, or work it around your own rhythms. I'm not a morning person, so my work hours are 12 – 6 pm and only on weekdays. That way, I'm not running myself into the ground trying to work at all hours. One of my colleagues found that when she set business hours, rather than meeting with clients any time from 7 am to 7 pm and wearing herself out, her business actually became more successful.

  Make sure that you maintain a healthy diet, get exercise and enough sleep. Take breaks and vacations – you'll be more productive in the long run when you're healthy and well-rested. Mark off time in your calendar and don't schedule appointments – or answer business calls, emails and texts – during that time.

- **Isolation** – If you're working alone, build social connections. Go to networking events, meet regularly with colleagues and have a social life. If it's appropriate, you might share an office space with a colleague or rent an office in a coworking space, so there are always other people around to connect with between appointments.

- **Support system** — As the boss, you may be a one-person business. If you do have employees, you don't always want to share your concerns with them. Have your own support system, whether it's a coach or a trusted peer group that you can consult with about your business.

- **Getting clients** — Marketing is a necessary "evil" of having a business. This may come easily to you, or you may hate or fear it. In some professions, you need to personally connect with your potential clients. In other cases, you can hire a salesperson or marketing professional to do the selling for you. In some cases, well-placed ads or listings on professional websites or insurance panels can bring you a steady flow of clients. (More on marketing in chapter 5.)

- **Risk tolerance** – Some people love the excitement of jumping in, while others need to be safe and cautious. Honor your risk tolerance. If you push yourself to the point that you're terrified, you're not going to function optimally and it's not going to serve your business.

- **Being prepared/anticipating errors** – Make sure to do your due diligence before you jump in. Know what you're getting into, so you can go in with your eyes open and prepare for any obstacles that may come up.

  Be prepared to deal with mistakes – as diligent as you are, you can't anticipate everything that could happen, especially when you're new at this. There's a learning curve, and you won't always get it right. Have a financial cushion and a plan, and educate yourself about your profession and how to run a business, but be prepared to clean up a mess and change course when things go awry.

- **Staying focused and handling distractions** – In the beginning, excitement and adrenaline will carry you through. But you need to stay motivated after the initial excitement wears off and reality sets in. Be prepared for those moments of discouragement, frustration or boredom. Stay connected with your motivation or mission for doing this business, and get the support you need, whether from a coach, business partner or support group. (See chapter 3 for more about connecting with your motivation and mission.)

- **Managing yourself alongside the business** – Be prepared to keep the business going when personal issues come up. We all have difficult times in our life, but we can't let them distract us from our responsibilities to our clients.

    In most cases, if you're not serving clients, you will not get paid, unless you have staff or sub-contractors who can cover for you. If you're selling products, your distributors may be able to keep the momentum going even when you're not available. Any "personal days" you take are on you. Have a backup plan or have an honest conversation with your clients. If you can't fulfill your agreements, be prepared to reimburse them.

    Years ago, I hired someone to market one of my books. After I paid him, he ended up in a painful divorce and completely neglected my book. Needless to say, I never used him again. Not a good way to maintain a business.

This may seem like a lot to think about, but with some forethought, all of these things can be managed successfully. Take time to prepare and educate yourself, rather than jumping blindly into your business. As I said, excitement will carry you just so far. After that, you need to have a good foundation and a good work ethic in place.

On the other hand, don't procrastinate forever out of fear. Many of our fears come from our self-talk. We tell ourselves all kinds of discouraging stories about how we're not good enough or we scare ourselves with statistics about the market. But in my experience, when someone is excited about and committed to their work, they can move heaven and earth and, with patience and persistence, make it a success.

> "There's no scarcity of opportunity to make a living at what you love. There is only scarcity of resolve to make it happen."
> ~ Wayne Dyer

It also helps to get the proper support. You may have people around you who discourage you from taking the leap, either out of concern or jealousy. You don't need that. Keep your plans to yourself until they're on solid ground, and share them only with people who will support and encourage you, who are truly happy for your success. Find an entrepreneurial or "mastermind" group – a group of trusted professionals who meet on a regular basis to support each other's businesses. Find people who have a positive outlook and can be trusted to keep your business issues confidential.

Some aspects of running a business will be new to you. These can be learned or delegated. There are numerous books and classes on starting a business and marketing (including this one!) that can teach you what you need to know. You can also get support from other professionals, such as a life or small business coach, an accountant or bookkeeper, a virtual assistant, a web designer, a social media manager, etc. Figure out which parts of the business you enjoy or can manage with ease and where it would save you time and money to hire someone.

If getting clients is your concern, there are numerous marketing books for coaches* and other private practitioners. You can also find a coach, mentor or marketing professional who understands your business and can teach and support you in building your practice.

As I said earlier, you don't have to have a business degree to successfully start a professional practice. You just have to be committed, learn what you need to know and get the support you need. Having some passion or enthusiasm for what you do is also a big plus. In this book, my intent is to give you a guide to starting your practice that makes it feel doable, along with additional resources if you want or need to get deeper into any aspect.

Some of these concerns will be resolved with time. As you gain experience, you'll become more confident in your work and more self-assured about approaching potential clients. Running a business takes work, so why not set it up in a way that you can enjoy it!

Use the worksheet on the following pages to plan how you can address the challenges.

*My book, *Creative Marketing Tools for Coaches*, offers a lot of user-friendly tips for using your natural gifts to connect with clients.

Addressing the Challenges

Concerns I Need to Address

- Finances/losing the steady paycheck

- Fear

- Shift in identity/being the boss

- Owning responsibility

- Wearing multiple hats

- Creating structure and accountability

- Discipline/work ethic

- Balancing business with personal

- Isolation

Things I Can Do

_____
_____
_____
_____
_____
_____
_____
_____
_____
_____
_____
_____
_____
_____
_____
_____
_____
_____
_____
_____

Concerns I Need to Address

- Support system

- Getting clients

- Risk tolerance

- Being prepared/anticipating errors

- Staying focused/handling distractions

- Managing yourself alongside the business

- _____

- _____

- _____

Things I Can Do

_____
_____
_____
_____
_____
_____
_____
_____
_____
_____
_____
_____
_____
_____
_____
_____
_____
_____
_____
_____
_____
_____
_____
_____
_____

Managing the Transition

As you transition into your new business, I'd like to support you in minimizing the risks involved. In the next chapter, we'll start creating a plan for your business. For now, let's look at some ways you can ease the transition.

⬥ **Be clear on your vision for the business**

I've found that when people are clear on what they want and why they want it, they move ahead with greater confidence.

- Work your business plan
- Have realistic goals
- Be clear on your branding

We'll work on this in the next chapter.

⬥ **Crunch the numbers**

As you transition into your new business, you need to know that you can pay your bills. Being in a place of financial insecurity is not conducive to a positive experience, and potential clients can "smell" desperation when you try to enroll them.

Unless you're seeking loans or investments, it's not necessary to do a full-blown formal business plan, but you do want to have a sense of what you need financially as you start your business.

- Do a budget and/or income/expense projections (see page 64 for an example)
- Determine how long you'll need to maintain another income stream or how much savings you need to cover your expenses until the business becomes profitable
- Be prepared to finance the start-up phase with savings, loans or investors

⬥ **Prepare**

The more prepared you are, the more confident you'll be and the less fear you'll experience. If you have a high risk tolerance and not a lot of responsibilities, go for it. But for most of us, knowing what we're getting into helps us to have a smoother transition and a greater chance of long-term success, while minimizing fear and anxiety.

- Make sure you understand what you need to start the business – skills, equipment, finances, etc.
- Learn how to reach your target market

- Acquire any new skills and information you need to work with clients and to run a business, or find help
- Connect with colleagues and resources, so you have a good support system

◇ Create a transition plan

While you may favor a spontaneous approach, I highly recommend having some kind of plan or structure to keep yourself on track, rather than floundering for months or years and wasting precious time.

> "If you fail to plan, you are planning to fail!"
> ~ Benjamin Franklin

Some things to think about:

- Will you continue in your current job? For how long?
- Can you work part-time until your business gets off the ground?
- Will you continue to have other income streams?
- How will you structure your time to include work with clients, marketing, developing materials, personal time, etc.?
- Will you need to make changes in your lifestyle to accommodate your new business? Is your family on board with that?

◇ Be patient and persistent

There's a saying, "Don't quit five minutes before the miracle." Starting a business takes a concerted effort. There may be times when it doesn't look like it will happen.

I often hear people say, "If I'm not successful in (#) years, I'll quit and just get another job." There may be a good reason for that. But to my mind, going in with a don't–quit attitude is much more powerful than keeping your eye on the exit door.

When I left my last job to focus full-time on my coaching business, it took two years before it "kicked in" and I started making a living from my business. It's been 20+ years since then that I've been able to enjoy working for myself. If I had quit, that never would have happened.

Remember …

- Launching a business takes time
- Have realistic expectations, and …
- Don't give up!

Chapter 3: Creating a Vision and Brand for Your Business

For a business that's applying for loans or courting investors, you would need to do a full-blown business plan, which includes your vision for the business, among many other things. Even for a solo practice that you're funding yourself, it's important to have a vision, so you know where you're heading and can plan and prepare in order to minimize the risk and increase your chance of success. And it doesn't hurt to envision a business that will make you happy.

At this point, I like to make a distinction between an "entrepreneur" and a "propreneur" (a term coined by Paul and Sarah Edwards). An **entrepreneur** is someone who loves business and finds a product or service that their business can provide. A **propreneur** is a professional who needs to start a business in order to sell their services or products, but doesn't necessary love running a business. The distinction is in the underlying motivation.

As a propreneur, in order to maximize your time and value, you'll want to be clear on which parts of the business you will handle yourself and which parts you'll hire out. My feeling is that, if you're starting a business, you want to set it up in a way that you can enjoy doing what you love and that you're good at, and not get bogged down doing parts of the business that could be handled more efficiently and cost-effectively by hiring a professional in that area.

As you envision your professional practice, keep in mind how you want to design your business. There are no "shoulds" here. It's about what will make you happy and allow you to thrive in your work and your life. It's not always about making it bigger. One of my clients envisioned a growing business with employees and even franchises in the future, but later decided to keep it small and do what she could do herself. The best plan is the one that supports your values and needs. I don't want to manage people, so I work solo. I'm not a morning person, so I designed my workday to start at noon. That way, I'm awake and refreshed as I talk to clients, teach or work on my books.

Best case scenario, you'll do what you love and delegate the parts you don't like, or aren't good at, to other professionals. I happen to find balancing my checkbook relaxing. If you don't, a virtual assistant or bookkeeper you can trust would be a good investment. If you're technologically challenged, having someone create and manage your website could save you a lot of wear and tear. If you hate social media, hiring a social media manager would take that burden off your plate. You might hire a virtual assistant (VA) who can handle a variety of tasks for you.

In many cases, it's more cost-effective to spend money on outside vendors to handle chores that you might not do well, that would sap a lot of your time and energy that would be better spent working on money-making activities. You don't want to waste valuable time doing things you hate or aren't good at — especially when you can have someone do those tasks at a lower rate than you charge for your services. Better to free yourself up to make more money that would pay for those services and then some.

Designing Your Business to Support Your Needs and Desires

Let's begin by looking at your goals for your business. Note that the work you do here will feed into a business plan that you'll work on in chapter 4.

◆ **Purpose or Mission**

Having your own business may seem like a way to get out of a job or career you don't enjoy, but it is a commitment. If you're not committed to the purpose of your work, you'll burn out or get discouraged pretty quickly. Many practitioners start their own business because they want to serve in some way or use a skill or talent that they love and are good at. For others, having their own practice gives them more flexibility and control, more freedom to pursue a passion or more time with their loved ones.

What is the purpose of your business?

One way of articulating your purpose is through a **Mission Statement**. A Mission Statement is a succinct statement that encapsulates the purpose or mission of your business.

Here's an example of mine:

> *The mission of Good Life Coaching is to support motivated adults to create a vision for a life that authentically reflects their passions and values, and then to support them in fearlessly achieving that vision.*

Use the worksheet on the following page to work out your Mission Statement. For some examples, go to MissionStatements.com, or try the Mission Statement Builder at FranklinCovey.com. Once you've honed and polished it, you may want to put it on your bulletin board or other places where you can see it when you need inspiration.

Mission Statement

What is the purpose of your business? What do you get from working on this business? What will you contribute to your clients, the community or society?

How does this business reflect your values? What are you passionate about?

How will this business contribute to your life and lifestyle? How will you grow as a person or practitioner as a result of this business?

Put your answers together to create a Mission Statement that excites and inspires you.

◆ **Services and Products**

Next, think about the services and products that you would like to offer. Even if your business is service-oriented, you may also create products for passive income. I work a lot with life coaches, and many of them create books, e-books, audios, videos and self-study programs to draw in clients with items at a lower price point than their services and create an additional stream of income. These can also provide extra income when sold "back of room" at speaking engagements and workshops – which are great ways to connect with potential clients. If you're selling products, you might offer services that teach people how to use them more effectively. (More about marketing in chapter 5.)

As your business evolves, you may add additional services or products. This is a great way to stay fresh and engaged and respond to changes in the marketplace. Many practitioners get additional certifications to add services that will enhance their ability to help their clients. For example, as a coach or therapist, you may want to learn hypnotherapy or EFT tapping to help your clients overcome blocks and obstacles. As a web designer, you might want to learn how to write strong marketing copy and how to structure websites to have the greatest impact.

Use the worksheet on the following page to list the services and products that you would like to offer. Think ahead – remember, you don't have to launch everything at once.

Services and Products

My professional services:

My products:

◆ **Your Target Audience**

Many practitioners feel they need to be open to anyone who might use their services. They don't want to limit themselves. Ultimately, you can work with anyone who's a good match for you, but in order to effectively market your business, you need to have a focused brand, which includes being clear on who are the clients or customers who will be most attracted to your products or services and who you will most enjoy working with.

Here are some examples:

- As a life coach, your ideal client may be "working mothers who are struggling with work/life balance" or "mid-life adults who want to clarify the next stage of their career."
- As a graphic designer, you may specialize in print or web design, packaging, direct mail, etc. You may target large corporations or entrepreneurs, or specialize in certain industries or a unique style.
- As a professional organizer, your sweet spot may be homes or business offices. You might employ the principles of feng shui. You might further specialize in designing and organizing small apartments or tiny houses, or staging homes to enhance their salability.
- As a massage therapist, you may enjoy working with athletes or pregnant women or those who want a particular type of massage, such as Swedish, deep tissue or shiatsu.

You're not limited to only serving clients in your preferred niche, but knowing your ideal client profile helps you to focus your marketing. I've also found that when you target clients you enjoy, you and your business are more likely to thrive.

Use the worksheet on the following page to create a description of your ideal client base. Use whichever attributes are relevant for your profession.

My Ideal Clients

For personal or professional services:

Age range:

Gender expression:

Profession:

Need or situation that aligns with your services:

Characteristic(s)/personality type (e.g., motivated, easy-going, courageous, creative, etc.):

For projects:

Types of projects:

Length of projects (e.g., short-term vs long-term):

Price/quality range (e.g., high-end luxury to low-end affordable):

Characteristics of clients I like to work with (e.g., easy to work with, appreciate innovation, know what they want, imaginative, open to new ideas, etc.)

Anything else:

◆ Marketability

In my experience, when you're passionate about and committed to your work, have a skill that's needed in the marketplace, do the necessary preparation, learn how to market effectively and then market persistently, you will be successful at it.

Some people feel more confident knowing for sure that they have a viable product or service. For a propreneur, it's probably not cost-effective to hire a market research firm. Instead, look at trends in the marketplace. Peruse the media for articles relevant to your profession. Join a professional association and talk to those who are already successful at what you want to do.

You can also speak to people in your target market or run a survey on social media or Survey Monkey. Find out:

- What are their needs? Why would they hire you or purchase your products?
- Are they willing to pay for your services or products to meet those needs?
- How much are they willing to pay? Do they see the value of what you're offering?

Look at your competitors. Study their websites. How do you feel about the way they present themselves? What do you like? Dislike? Use this information to begin to formulate how you can present yourself so that you stand out in the marketplace and attract the clients you want. We'll talk later in this chapter about designing a brand.

◆ Pricing Your Services and Products

Before you speak to prospective clients, you'll need to work out the pricing structure for your services and products, as best as you can at this point. To price products, look at the going rates for similar products. Determine whether you want your products to be perceived as high-end, affordable or somewhere in between. Of course, the quality of the product needs to match your pricing strategy. What do you need to charge to make your business profitable? Is there something unique that will make your products or services stand out in the marketplace and command a higher price? Consult with mentors in your industry to set the optimal prices, so that your products and services will sell and also enable you to build a viable business.

Pricing for services in particular can be fluid, but you want to have a clear starting point that you can confidently communicate to potential clients. As the demand for your services and your proficiency increase, or as the market shifts, you can adjust your pricing accordingly. Some entrepreneurs like to reassess on an annual basis.

Professional rates are industry-specific. Pricing and packages for life coaches, for example, can be all over the board. I recommend that you research pricing within your industry, geographic area (although many services can now be done virtually), level of experience and the ability of your target audience to pay. Consult with your teachers and mentors for guidance. Remember, you can always adjust your prices as you gain experience and become more in demand.

If you're experienced and confident in your work, you can start out with a pricing structure that reflects the value of your work.

Many of my coaching students who are just starting out feel nervous about asking for a high rate, or even charging for their services at all. Don't fall into the trap of undervaluing what you're offering or even giving it away for free. People often don't value what they don't pay for. Even if you're just starting, your services and products help people, and you deserve to be paid for them.

If you're new and just building your confidence, here are some strategies:

- Transition your practice (pro bono) clients from your training program to paying clients by negotiating a fee or donation.
- DO NOT set your prices low and suddenly double them. Starting with the rates you truly want to charge and discounting them for a period of time (if needed) sits better with clients, who will appreciate getting a deal rather than suddenly paying escalating prices.
- Set the rates that you would like to get. Then, if you feel uncomfortable and/or are trying to build a practice from the ground up and just want to get clients fast, offer a discount. For example, you might offer a 50% discount for the first package or time period, 25% for the next one, and then go up to your full rate. By then, if your clients keep renewing, you'll know that you're doing a good job and giving value. You'll have more experience under your belt and greater confidence about charging higher rates.
- Offer discounted rates or do some pro bono work for deserving clients in order to create portfolio pieces to show off your work. If you're exploring your brand, invite clients in your proposed niche to work with you, so you can see if this target audience works well for you.
- Set a schedule for your practice – for example, 3 clients per day, Tuesday, Wednesday and Thursday afternoons – and fill those spots with pro bono and paying clients. As you gain more paying clients, let the pro bono clients go or transition them to paying clients. If there are expenses related to your practice (e.g., acupuncture supplies or workbooks), you might just charge pro bono clients enough to cover your expenses.

I recommend that you *not* publish your rates, at least at first, so you have room to negotiate a higher fee, or offer a discount, without being held to your published rates.

If your services are complex, or if you're selling to businesses, you may need to learn how to write a project proposal for each prospective client. Consult with an experienced mentor or the following resources:

- *Persuasive Business Proposals*, by Tom Sant
- *Million Dollar Consulting Proposals*, by Alan Weiss
- *Proposal Best Practices*, by David Seibert

Use the worksheet on the following page to work out your pricing.

Pricing Plan for My Business

FIll in whichever items are relevant for your business.

Services:

Hourly rate:

Package or project rates (e.g., 3 months, 20 hours, 5-page website, etc.):

Retainer rate and what's included:

Rates for various services:

- _____ $_____
- _____ $_____
- _____ $_____
- _____ $_____
- _____ $_____
- _____ $_____

Products:

- _____ $_____
- _____ $_____
- _____ $_____
- _____ $_____
- _____ $_____
- _____ $_____

◆ **Your Work Schedule**

You'll need to plan your work schedule to accommodate the income you want to produce, your pricing structure, as well as what's practical in terms of how many clients you can work with at a time. If you're a high-energy person, you may thrive on a packed schedule. If you find yourself feeling drained by the end of the day, you'll need to limit the number of clients you see or the amount of work you can accomplish per day. Remember, you also need to leave time for administrative and marketing activities, unless you can hire others to do that for you, as well as taking care of yourself and having a personal life.

If you're working on a project basis, figure out how many projects you can manage at the same time. To grow your business, you might hire others to do some parts of the business to free you up to do the more money-making activities that use your best (and most lucrative) skills and talents.

Remember to include personal time in your schedule. You may find yourself working 18-hour days out of passion or fear. Either way, that will wear you down eventually. Be sure to make time for sleep, exercise, preparing healthy meals, time with friends and family, as well as activities that feed your soul (besides your business, if that's a labor of love). And it doesn't hurt to have some open, unscheduled time that you can use however you want.

Use the worksheet on the following page to map out a schedule. You might color-code different activities.

My Work Schedule

Here's a sample ...

	Monday	Tuesday	Wednesday	Thursday	Friday	Saturday	Sunday
7 - 8 am	Meditate & Shower	Meditate & Shower	Meditate & Shower	Meditate & Shower			
8 - 9 am	Breakfast	Breakfast	Breakfast	Breakfast			
9 - 10 am	Clients	Clients	Clients	Clients	Meditate & Shower	Meditate & Shower	Meditate & Shower
10 - 11 am					Breakfast	Breakfast	Breakfast
11 am - 12 pm					Marketing and Admin	House and Shopping	Family time
12 - 1 pm	Lunch	Lunch	Lunch	Lunch			
1 - 2 pm	Walk	Read	Walk	Read			
2 - 3 pm	Clients	Clients	Clients	Clients	Lunch	Lunch	Lunch
3 - 4 pm					Walk		Walk
4 - 5 pm		Gym		Gym		Gym	Family time
5 - 6 pm							
6 - 7 pm	Dinner	Dinner	Dinner	Dinner	Dinner		
7 - 8 pm	Family time	Family time	Family time	Family time	Family time	Dinner	Dinner
8 - 9 pm							
9 - 10 pm	Read	Read	Read	Read			
10 - 11 pm	Bedtime	Bedtime	Bedtime	Bedtime	Bedtime	Bedtime	Bedtime

Now do yours ...

	Monday	Tuesday	Wednesday	Thursday	Friday	Saturday	Sunday
6 - 7 am							
7 - 8 am							
8 - 9 am							
9 - 10 am							
10 - 11 am							
11 am - 12 pm							
12 - 1 pm							
1 - 2 pm							
2 - 3 pm							
3 - 4 pm							
4 - 5 pm							
5 - 6 pm							
6 - 7 pm							
7 - 8 pm							
8 - 9 pm							
9 - 10 pm							
10 - 11 pm							
11 pm - 12 am							

◆ Personnel

Many propreneurs are solo practitioners, but you may still need to work with a web designer; graphic designer; accountant or bookkeeper; copywriter, editor or proofreader; assistant or virtual assistant or others to support your business. You may even sub-contract with others in your profession to take on additional clients or to take on parts of bigger projects and expand your potential. These folks will most likely be independent contractors, to whom you pay a designated fee, but no benefits.

If you do take on staff, you'll need to set up payroll, taxes and health insurance for them. Work with your accountant or consult the Small Business Association (sba.gov) to make sure you're complying with tax requirements for your situation. Note that staff are usually people who work for you as employees, usually on your premises, while independent contractors often have their own businesses and work from their own premises using their own equipment. Since the pandemic, you may have employees who work from home full- or part-time (hybrid). Check with your accountant or lawyer to ensure that you're complying with state and federal regulations in classifying these workers as employees vs. independent contractors.

Another option is to have a business partner. In this case, it's especially important to craft your vision together and make sure that you have the same goals and level of commitment. Even if you've known this person for years, business partnership is like a marriage, and you'll probably learn things about each other that you didn't know. It can be fun and exciting to dream up a business with someone, but once you get "into the trenches," a lack of clarity and alignment, especially where finances and allocation of responsibilities are concerned, and differing goals and visions for the business can turn into messy fights. Be sure to have a written agreement with your partner; you may also want to establish a legal partnership or corporation together.

Here's a resource for that:

Business Partnership Essentials: A Step-by-Step Action Plan for Succeeding in Business With a Partner, by Dorene Lehavi, PhD

Use the worksheet on the following page to consider what types of people you might need to support your business.

People I Need to Support My Business

Business partner(s):

Staff/Outside vendors/Independent contractors:

- Accountant
- Bookkeeper
- Website Designer/Manager
- Marketing/Social Media
- Assistant/Virtual Assistant
- Copywriter/Editor/Proofreader
- Lawyer
- _____
- _____
- _____

Others in my field to whom I can subcontract additional clients or tasks:

- _____
- _____
- _____

Your Vision and Goals

It's also helpful to have a vision or intention for your business – the intangible part of your plan. From that vision, you can draw out goals and plans.

What is it that you want to accomplish with your work, for yourself and others?

Many people are motivated by having something to reach for. Your goals may be income goals, achievement goals or a level of personal satisfaction from using your gifts and talents or responding to a creative or spiritual calling. Each person is motivated differently, so find what motivates you personally to commit to building your practice.

For example, what's motivated me is my passion for personal and spiritual growth and the desire to contribute the wisdom I've gained from my own learning and experiences to help others live an inspired life.

> "Dare to dream! If you did not have the capability to make your wildest wishes come true, your mind would not have the capacity to conjure such ideas in the first place. There is no limitation on what you can potentially achieve, except for the limitation you choose to impose on your own imagination. What you believe to be possible will always come to pass – to the extent that you deem it possible. It really is as simple as that."
> ~ Anthon St. Maarten

Have fun creating your vision. Don't hold back – dream big!

> "Shoot for the moon. Even if you miss, you'll land among the stars."
> ~ Les Brown

Use the worksheet on the following page to create a vision for your business.

Dream Big!

What excites you about your business?

What would you like to accomplish for yourself and others?

What is your wildest dream for your business (and your life)? What have you been too embarrassed to share with even your closest friends?

What will your life be like if you can achieve this?

Once you have an overall vision, you can start to home in on specific, tangible goals.

◆ Structure

As you think about your workday, what would you like that day to look like?

Do you see yourself working alone or with others? Are the "others" coworkers and/or clients?

Are you working from home or do you go to an office every day, or some combination? Do you go to your clients or do they come to you, or do you meet virtually?

What days of the week do you work? What are your business hours? Be careful of scheduling clients whenever they want, or you may find yourself working all hours of the day and burning out.

Do you spend your day in front of a computer, meeting with people, out in the field or something else?

Think about how you can structure your workday so that it supports both your business and your personal well-being.

◆ Size and expansion

Many people assume that when you start a business, you want to keep making it bigger. That's not true for everyone. You may want to stay a solopreneur and use outside vendors for tasks that you can't or don't want to do. You may work with one or two other people, or you may want to grow your start-up into a larger enterprise.

Whatever you choose, honor what's right for you. Remember that involving more people expands your potential, but it also means more responsibility and greater possibility for disagreements and conflicts, as well as needing to replace people who move on. You also want to keep in mind the lifestyle that you want. If you've chosen to start your own business in order to have more time freedom and flexibility, growing your business may make even greater demands on your time and energy. If your vision is to do something grand, go for it!

Be realistic about what you want, and do whatever research you need to do, so that you know what you're taking on and don't find yourself in over your head in the future.

> "One of the greatest tragedies in life is to lose your own sense of self and accept the version of you that is expected by everyone else."
> ~ K.L. Toth

At this point, you may not be clear on what you ultimately want for your practice. You may need to just dive in, take the first steps, and as you clarify each piece, the greater vision will emerge. Start with short-term goals and expand them as your vision opens up.

In any case, make sure your plan is realistic. If you have the resources to quit your day job and focus solely on your new practice, go for it. If not, or if you want to move slowly to minimize the risk, start with a short-term plan and take it step by step. As the business unfolds, your vision will emerge.

The Vision Statement

One way to begin your plan is with a Vision Statement. This may include the type of work you do, the clients you work with, where you work, colleagues or others who support your business, how much you work, the income you make, the joy you get from your work, a typical work day, as well as the lifestyle that comes with it – how you spend your time outside of work.

Here's an example:

My therapy practice brings me joy every day. Helping young people work through their issues and open up to a brighter future is immensely gratifying. I see 5 wonderful clients a day, 5 days a week. I have an abundant income of at least $125,000 and an assistant to handle the required paperwork and book appointments for me. I take engaging continuing education classes that help me to continue developing professionally and having greater resources to help my clients.

Because I love my work so much, my stress is minimal. My schedule allows me to have a balanced life. I have time to take yoga classes 3 times a week and spend plenty of quality time with my family and friends. I take 2 wonderful vacations a year, including one trip abroad. I have time to read great books, go to theatre and movies and take a painting class to develop my passion for landscape art. And all of this is accompanied by my beloved pooch.

Use the worksheets on the following pages to work out your vision and goals for your business.

My Vision Statement

Write a vision statement for your business (and lifestyle).

Goals for My Business

What I want to accomplish during the start-up phase:

- _____
- _____
- _____
- _____
- _____

Goals for the first year:

- _____
- _____
- _____
- _____
- _____

Long-term goals:

- _____
- _____
- _____
- _____
- _____

Defining Your Brand

Before you do anything else, it's important to get clear on how you want to define and present your business. This is your corporate identity – more commonly called your "branding." Your marketing efforts will rest on having a clear, compelling brand that will attract your ideal clients.

Branding includes:

- The services and/or products you provide
- Your target audience
- What sets you apart from your competitors
- How you want to be perceived by your client base

Your branding will impact your choice of business name; the colors, words and graphics that you'll use on your website and promotional materials; and even how you dress when engaging with potential clients. You might even use a fun, creative title for yourself that aligns with your brand, such as "Image Consultant to the Stars" or "The Organizing Ninja."

If you've done the work in the previous chapter, you've already clarified your services, products and target audience.

So now, let's look at what sets you apart from your competition. Most likely, you're not the only one in your market doing what you do, so you need to communicate to potential clients why you may be the best one to fulfill their particular needs. This is called your Unique Selling Point (USP). As a service provider, your USP may be a combination of your credentials, training and education; personal and professional experience; talents, personal qualities and strengths; and the types of people or companies you work best with. If you're selling a product, be prepared to explain why your product is better or different than that of your competitors.

Use the worksheet on the following pages to work out your branding.

What Makes Me and My Business Unique?

◆ **My credentials, training and education:**

◆ **Services and products I offer:**

◆ **My professional experiences:**

What experiences have you had that set you apart? What is your skill set? Have you had advanced training in an area that's in demand? Specialized in a particular population? Been mentored by someone well-known in your field? Developed a unique product or service?

◆ **My personal experiences:**

What have you experienced personally that helps you to connect with and understand your clients? Have you experienced what you're helping clients with? Is there a challenge you've overcome? Do you have a relevant hobby or volunteer experience?

◆ **Personal qualities and strengths that make me stand out:**

What qualities do you have – things you may take for granted – that would be attractive and valuable to your clients? Are you a great listener? Empathetic? Skilled in a particular area? Known for getting results with a challenging problem? For making people comfortable?

◆ **My message:**

Aside from your niche and target audience, do you have a unique message that will draw clients to you? What led you to this business? Some of my coaching students help their clients live an adventurous life, thrive as a late bloomer, rebuild their life after an illness or injury, etc. What's your story and how will your clients relate? How do you inspire your clients?

◆ **My ideal client profile**

Who do you work best with? A particular age group or gender expression? People who've had a particular life experience? Qualities you enjoy, such as creative, curious or collaborative? People in an industry that you've worked in? Do you have credentials that qualify you to get great results with a particular issue? Think about who you have easy access to, as well as the types of clients you most enjoy working with.

Elevator Speech

One way to get really clear on your message is to develop an Elevator Speech. Because it's short and focused, you really have to distill your message to its essence – a statement that your target audience will immediately relate to and be excited by.

An Elevator Speech is usually spoken to someone face-to-face, so it should be succinct and easy to say and understand. For example:

- I work with acupuncture to help my clients overcome chronic pain that no other health practitioner has been able to help them with before.
- I'm a Career Coach. I work with my clients to discover a career path that they're excited about every day.
- Do you know how so many small-business owners dread doing bookkeeping? I take that chore off their plate and allow them to focus on the parts of their business that they enjoy, while making sure that their finances are in order.

Notice that the Elevator Speech is short and to-the-point. It should be something that people can easily understand and relate to. You don't want it to be overloaded with extraneous details, overused buzz words, processes or jargon that get people lost in figuring out what you said. Here's a bad example:

- I'm a Life Coach and I empower my clients to have the life they've always dreamed of and to fulfill their highest potential by helping them create a vision, and then set goals and take action steps to achieve them.

How exciting is that??

Practice saying your Elevator Speech out loud, so that it flows and sounds naturalå, rather than sounding like you're reciting a memorized speech. Once you've captured someone's attention, you can have your talking points ready to give them more information, but don't throw them all into the Elevator Speech and overwhelm your prospect.

Use the worksheet on the following page to craft one or more Elevator Speeches.

Elevator Speech

Write one or more Elevator Speeches that will catch the attention of your ideal clients. You can have a separate one for each issue, challenge or type of client you might be addressing.

Section 11: Launching Your Business

Starting a professional practice isn't as complicated as starting a business that includes employees, manufacturing, distribution, etc. As a solo practitioner, you'll most likely work on your own, perhaps with the help of an assistant or virtual assistant, web/graphic designer, accountant and other supporters who function as independent contractors. At most, you might have one or two employees or a small group of sub-contractors. (See page 35 for more on Personnel.)

In this section, we'll look at what you need to do to get your business going. In the following section, we'll look at the ongoing operation of your business.

Chapter 4: The Nuts and Bolts of Business Start-Up

Now that you've got a vision in place, let's look at the steps you'll need to take to get your business going – what I call the "nuts and bolts."

Compliance, Ethics, Licensing, Certification and Insurance Panels

Before you do anything else, be sure that you are aware of any licensing or certification requirements for your profession. In some cases, licensing may be required in order to practice legally. In others, getting one or more certifications or professional credentials may be advantageous to enhance your skills and credibility. In my profession, life coaching, anyone can call themselves a coach, but the public are becoming wiser and looking for coaches with training, credentials and experience. Corporations that hire coaches often require an advanced degree and/or a credential from the International Coaching Federation.

You'll also need to be aware of ethical and compliance requirements. For example, if you're a licensed psychotherapist, you may need to run your promotional materials by your insurance provider to make sure you're not crossing any lines. Many professional organizations have a code of ethics. It's wise to abide by that code to be a trusted professional. In some cases, violating your professional organization's code of ethics can result in a financial penalty, loss of your license or even imprisonment if a client experiences damage from your services. (See more about liability insurance on page 59.)

Also, find out what you need to do to operate your business legally in your state and/or country. Aside from professional licensing, you may need to officially establish your business by registering a "dba" (doing business as), registering a fictitious or assumed name, or even establishing a corporation. If you're selling products, you'll need to register for, collect and pay sales tax to your state. Consult your state's website or a qualified lawyer or accountant to make sure that you have the proper paperwork in place. If you don't, you could incur serious penalties, so take the time to set your business up correctly.

If the service you provide is covered by insurance, you may want to look into getting onto some insurance panels to connect with potential clients. This may involve a lot of paperwork and reduced fees, so run the numbers to see if it's beneficial to get on these panels. One practitioner I know found it was beneficial to be on several panels and have a busy practice, and to hire someone to handle the paperwork for her.

Choosing a Business Name and Professional Title

Your **business name** can be your name or one that describes or portrays what you do. Some people like a straightforward name, like Get-It-Done Graphics or Feel Good Massage. Others enjoy having a name that expresses the feeling of what they do, such as Joyful Life Coaching. Maybe it's something more creative and evocative, like Soar to Success Executive Coaching.

In some cases, such as a medical practitioner, you can keep it simple and just use your name, perhaps with a tag line to express the spirit of your practice (e.g., A healthy life is a happy life!). If you want to become known as a speaker/author, you'll want to create a brand around your name.

Important: Whatever name you choose, make sure it reflects your brand and use it consistently!

In working with my coaching students, I've seen many people choose a name that they loved, but it didn't explain the focus or the purpose of their work. If you choose an unusual name, be sure to explain upfront (i.e., on your homepage) how that name relates to your work. You don't want to leave people so confused that they just leave your website.

If a name doesn't come to you naturally, brainstorm some ideas. Come up with a list of keywords that express what you do and the feeling you want people to get from your website and promotional materials, and then combine them in different ways. Try brainstorming with other people. Group energy often generates great ideas.

Come up with as many ideas as you can. Then put the list away. Look at it again in a few days and pick out the ones that feel good to you. Put it away and come back to it a few days later. Continue the process until you have a few names that you like.

Once you have a few desirable options, check them out in two places:

- Make sure that the domain name (URL) for your website is available. You can test names at any do-it-yourself website host, such as godaddy.com, bluehost.com, squarespace.com or wix.com. I often use www.dotster.com or www.namecheap.com to check the availability of a domain. If your name is taken, they suggest other options, although some of them can be pretty off-track.

If you're not sure yet where you want to host your website, don't worry. If you find a domain name that you like, just lock it in for a year for a small investment; you can move it to another host at a later time. If you find several names that are available, reserve all of them for a year, so you have time to decide. You don't want to land on a name you love, only to come back to it and find that the domain has been taken.

If the .com is taken, you can also use a .biz, .org, .net or other suffix, but be aware that .com is the most common, so there may be some confusion if you use another suffix, especially if the .com is owned by someone in your profession. You can try separating the words with hyphens, although it could be confusing if a search engine pulls up both you and your competitor. Play with different combinations until you find one you like that's available and doesn't bring up your competitors.

Note that there are companies that buy up desirable URLs and sell them for thousands of dollars. I don't recommend falling for this ploy, even if it takes more creativity to come up with something you like that's also available at a reasonable rate.

- If you're planning to register your business and/or incorporate, you need to make sure that your business name is available in your state. Your first step might be to google the name and see if it comes up. A more secure way is to to go your state website and find the procedure for searching business names.

Once you've confirmed that your name is available in both places, purchase your domain name to secure it, even if you're not ready to launch a website yet. (See page 54 for more on establishing your business structure.)

As far as your **professional title**, it may be inherent in your type of business: graphic designer, accountant, etc. With a profession like life coaching, you have more creative leeway. You might create a title that reflects your business name, such as Transition Coach, Parenting Coach, Creativity Coach, or even something whimsical like Inspiration Coach or Dream Creation Coach.

One thing I do NOT recommend is using President, Founder or Owner as your title. It doesn't reflect what you do and, if you use it on social media, you won't come up in a keyword search. If someone is searching for a bookkeeper, they're not going to be searching on "president."

On the following page, list ideas for your business name and professional title.

My Business Name and Professional Title

Write down your ideas for your business name – which will also reflect your website domain name – and your professional title. Explore ideas that clearly reflect the focus of your business and that also excite and inspire you. If you'd like, add a tag line that further clarifies your brand.

Setting Up Your Business Structure and Taxes

A business generally takes one of three forms:

- a sole proprietorship
- a partnership
- a corporation

If you're a solo practitioner, you may be able to start as a "sole proprietorship," or "dba" (doing business as). If you have one or more business partners, you'll need to set up a partnership or corporation. In any case, you may want to incorporate at some point for legal and/or tax reasons. Incorporating shields you (somewhat) from personal liability, but it also brings additional legal and tax liabilities, as well as the expense of doing an additional set of taxes for the business. (Income and expenses for a sole proprietorship can be claimed through your personal taxes.) (See more about liability insurance on page 59.)

I don't recommend rushing into incorporation, unless it's required or prudent for your profession. In many cases, you can do business under your own name or register a dba or fictitious name statement to get started.

If you feel ready to incorporate, consult with a lawyer or accountant who understands the ramifications of the process to determine whether it's beneficial at this time and which form is best for you. If you incorporate too soon, dissolving a company can cost you in time and fees. Make sure you're clear before you begin the incorporation process.

> *Tip: Find an accountant who's familiar with working with small businesses. You don't want someone who has a steep learning curve and who's learning on your time and your dime. Their mistakes can cost you. And don't be pressured into filing documents that your small business doesn't need (e.g., quarterly filings), so that your accountant can make more money.*

Many practitioners form an LLC (limited liability corporation), although your advisor may suggest an S-corporation. Both forms filter through your personal taxes, but you still need to file for the corporation as well. Your advisor should be familiar with the details of each option and which is best for your situation.

Once you set up your business, you'll need to get a **Federal Tax ID** (aka Employer Identification Number or EIN) for your corporation or partnership. If you're a sole proprietor, you can either function under your Social Security number or apply for an EIN for your business.

If you'll be selling goods, you'll also need to get a **Sales Tax ID** from your state. Once you do that, you will file and pay sales tax quarterly or annually, depending on the amount of taxable income from sales of merchandise. If you're purchasing goods that you will resell, you can give the vendor a **resale certificate**, which allows them to exempt you from paying their sales tax. Work with your accountant or state to determine what's needed. Don't skip this step. If you don't collect and pay sales tax for merchandise within your state, you will incur penalties.

Since you'll be collecting fees rather than a salary (which has various taxes deducted for you), you'll need to pay quarterly **Estimated Taxes**, both federal and, if applicable, state. You can download the forms from irs.gov and your state's website. Use their instructions to calculate the amount to pay or consult with your accountant. (FYI: If you're employed, your employer pays half the amount toward Social Security [FICA or OASDI]. As a self-employed person, you're responsible for the full amount. Again, talk to your accountant.)

When you're starting out, I recommend putting aside 20 – 25% of any payments you collect to cover Estimated Taxes and paying them quarterly. This is just an estimate, but 15% might go to the federal and 10% to the state. DO NOT wait until you file your taxes the following year to do this, as you will incur penalties. Once you get established and your income is fairly steady, your accountant should be able to pre-calculate your estimated taxes for the coming year and provide preprinted forms.

Once again, consulting with an accountant or tax attorney is crucial for this part of your business so that it's done correctly and you don't find yourself hit with penalties.

Writing a Basic Business Plan

For a business that requires loans or investors, a full-blown business plan will be required. You can get help from the Small Business Association (sba.gov) or SCORE (www.score.org) and their various local offices, a good business plan book or a professional business plan writer.

For a small or solo practitioner, it's not likely that you'll be pursuing investors (although you may get a small personal loan from your bank or credit union). You'll still want to have at least a basic business plan that addresses the key issues involved in starting a business, so that you have a clear vision and direction and are prepared for what's to come.

In chapter 3, you started creating a vision for your business. You've clarified:

- Purpose or mission
- Services and products
- Target audience

- Marketability
- Pricing structure
- Personnel
- Vision and goals
- Your brand

That work can go into your business plan. As you read ahead, we'll also be looking at plans for operations, finances, transitioning from your current situation and how you will market to reach your customers. All of these will inform your plan.

Operations

There are a number of things you need to put into place in order to operate your business.

Office or Work Space

To begin with, you need a place to run your business. This can be a home office or an outside space. Nowadays, many practitioners work remotely (other than bodyworkers, obviously!). In that case, you need a space that's comfortable and workable for you, with an attractive background for video meetings. You might want to invest in a green screen, so that you can have a professional-looking background of your choice without the wobble that you get without the green screen. (You might even create an attractive digital backdrop that includes your logo.) If you're doing creative work, whether hands-on or digital, you'll need a comfortable space to do your work and store your supplies.

If you'll be seeing clients in person, you need to have an appropriate professional space. Depending on your need, you can rent a full-time office or treatment room – which could be in a group wellness center or office suite that provides furniture and communal services such as reception, phones and utilities – or sublet by the hour from a colleague or a professional suite. Some practitioners, such as personal trainers and acupuncturists, can affiliate with a gym or wellness center, where you can access space part-time or full-time. If you have an appropriate space, you can see clients in your home.

If you're setting up your own office, you'll need to purchase furniture (desk, table, chairs, cabinets, bookshelves, filing, etc.), lighting and decoration, along with phone and Internet connections (although you can use your cell phone and get a mobile wi-fi connection). You may also need specialized equipment for your business, such as a massage table, exercise or medical equipment and a music system.

It goes without saying that you will need various forms of technology, such as a computer, printer, smart phone, tablet, wi-fi router, video equipment, sound system, etc. If you're renting space by the hour, you'll need mobile equipment, or you can find a space that provides at least some of the equipment or services that you need. Keep in mind that using someone else's wi-fi might not be safe for secure transactions.

If you're working from home, you may want to establish a post office box to receive mail, so that you don't have to publish your home address.

If your business includes the production of products, you'll need to find manufacturers, warehouses and distributors. Your industry colleagues and mentors will be able to suggest good vendors in these areas.

Client and Promotional Materials

Depending on your business, you may need to prepare materials for your clients. For example, as a life coach, mine include a client agreement, a welcome packet with various documents including a client information form and a credit card authorization form, as well as various worksheets that I use with my clients. You might need intake forms, questionnaires, project proposals or spec sheets. You can provide these on paper, as a PDF document that you can email or as fillable/downloadable online forms.

Every business should have letterhead, even if you mostly use it virtually. Use the same logo and fonts that you use on your website for consistency. While I rarely send letters anymore, I use my letterhead for digital proposals, class worksheets and invoices, among other things.

You will also most likely have a business card, as well as brochures, flyers, postcards or other promotional materials.

Recordkeeping and Taxes

You'll need a way to keep both financial and client records.

If your business is simple, you can use a basic program such as Quicken to manage your **personal and business income and expenses**. For more complex businesses, you can use a program such as Quickbooks, which has more functions, including invoicing and inventory.

You'll need to keep certain records for tax purposes. Be sure to keep records of payments you receive and business expenses. Unless you're subcontracting with companies who issue a 1099 or W-2 at the end of the year, you'll need to track your income on your own, so that you can report it accurately on your taxes.

Your payments from clients may come in the form of cash, checks, credit cards and online transfers. Unless you keep track yourself, only credit card receipts will be documented. It may be tempting to omit declaring cash payments, but it's important to operate your business ethically and establish yourself as a professional in the eyes of the government. You can only deduct business expenses up to the amount of your income from that profession. Remember, too, that your declared income will impact your rate of Social Security benefits down the line. You're never too young to plan for that! Your older self will appreciate your forethought.

As a professional, you can deduct expenses related to your profession from your taxable income, which will reduce your tax liability. Have your accountant help you set up categories in your accounting program, so that you can easily calculate the necessary figures. When you incur an expense, instead of throwing the receipt in a bag, log it into your program and tag it with the correct category. (Every time I get a credit card bill, I log the transactions into my Quicken account.) That way, at the end of the year, you can simply print out reports and hand them to your accountant. Do keep the receipts as a backup in case of an audit.

See page 77 for more about paying estimated taxes and collecting sales tax.

In some professions, you'll also need to keep **client records**. Some professions, such as licensed therapists and medical practitioners, will have prescribed guidelines to follow. If you're doing any other form of coaching, consulting or counseling, you can simply keep notes on what you covered in the session and any key points that came up.* Notes can simply be kept in a Word document, or you can use a practice management service (see page 82). If you're providing services such as graphic design, you might keep the client's previous work on file for updates. For services such as massage therapy (non-medical), client records are probably not necessary unless you want to keep notes for yourself on your regular clients' progress. For technology services, keep backups of your work.

Depending on your business, you may need to provide invoices or receipts to your clients. These can be set up in Quickbooks or you can create a receipt template in your word processing program, using your digital letterhead. If you're accepting credit card payments, Paypal or your credit card merchant accounts will generate email receipts. If you hire staff, you'll need to prepare W-2's (for salaried staff) or 1099s (for independent contractors) at the end of the year. When you hire them, employees will complete W-4's and contractors will submit W-9's. As always, check with your accountant for support on any financial and tax issues.

---

*Note: Life coaches' notes are not privileged in the way that therapists' notes are. I don't know anyone whose notes have been subpoenaed, but just be aware that they can be. You might include in your coaching agreement that any information the client shares will be held confidential "to the extent permitted by law."

Getting Help

As a propreneur, you're very likely a solopreneur, and you may need some support services. These can most likely be fulfilled by outside vendors or independent contractors. Some examples include web and graphic designers, copyeditors, bookkeepers and administrative assistants. If your administrative needs don't require the person to be in your office, virtual assistants can be very affordable.

For some tasks, it's cost-effective to hire help, rather than struggling with it yourself. One health practitioner I knew was spending a lot of time doing paperwork for insurance panels. The hourly rate of an assistant was much lower than her rate, and it freed her up to take on more business and make more money, which more than paid for the assistant. Even having someone for a few hours a week to check email, clear your spam filter, make appointments, update your website, invoice your clients, etc., can free up your time to focus on doing your money-making work.

At this point, there are many sources for finding assistants or virtual assistants. Ask your colleagues for recommendations, or look for referral services online. (See Resources, page 83.)

Insurance

Depending on your type of business and the extent of liability, you may need to carry various types of insurance. You'll certainly want to have health and perhaps disability insurance for yourself and your employees, if any. If you have one or more partners, it may be prudent to carry life insurance on each other, so that should something catastrophic happen, the survivor(s) will have resources to manage or close down the business.

Your profession may require some sort of liability or errors-and-omissions insurance. Do a web search or, even better, consult with professional colleagues and associations to get recommendations for reputable companies. Prices can vary widely, so do some comparison shopping.

If you're seeing clients in your home or office, you may want to have general liability insurance, as well as insuring the property and equipment. Some companies offer "small business insurance" that packages several types of insurance into one policy.

Bank Account

If you're functioning as a sole proprietor under your own name, you can deposit payments into your personal bank accounts. If you've established a business entity, you'll want to open a bank account in your business name. Once you register a sole proprietorship, partnership or corporation, you'll receive an official document that you can take to the bank to set up a business account. (See more about setting up a business entity on page 54.)

Accepting Payments

There are many ways that you can accept credit card payments. One simple way is to use Paypal. The advantage is that anyone can have a Paypal account, and you can accept payments from multiple currencies if your practice is international. The disadvantage is that you can request payment, but the client needs to put it through, so you lose some control if they're dragging their heels.

With your own credit card merchant accounts, you can keep clients' credit card information on file and put through payments as needed – with their authorization, of course. For example, many life coaches systematically charge their clients at the beginning of each month or for each new package. Square (www.squareup.com) is a popular system with no monthly or set-up fees; you just get charged fees per transaction.

If you see clients in person, there are several companies, including Paypal and Square, that offer devices and apps that you can use on smart phones and tablets, as well as point-of-sale equipment, to run credit card payments. Many of these companies charge a slightly lower fee if you swipe the actual credit card, as opposed to entering the information through their online portal. If you're meeting remotely with your clients, you can create an authorization form that you can keep on file that includes the information you need to process a payment. The client signs or authorizes verbally, giving you permission to put through payments as needed, with their permission. Be sure to file these securely.

Many do-it-yourself website hosts and practice management websites also include e-commerce options, including credit card processing. (See Practice Management resources on page 82.)

Zelle and Venmo are popular ways for clients to securely transfer money directly into your bank account.

And, of course, you can still accept cash and checks.

One caveat: I do NOT recommend allowing clients to run up a tab. If someone owes you hundreds of dollars, it can taint your professional relationship, and you don't want to waste your time and energy chasing down clients to get your money. Services should be paid for on the day they are provided, or clients can pre-purchase a package of sessions upfront.

Financial Plan

For many solopreneurs, the financial plan can be the most confronting aspect of planning their business. Budgeting may not be your strong point, but don't put blinders on and set yourself up for failure by ignoring this important piece. In most cases, it takes time for a business to start turning a profit, and you need to plan for how you'll pay your start-up expenses and ongoing bills as you build your clientele.

Unless you're applying for a loan or courting investors, it's unlikely that you'll need full-blown, formal financial projections. But you do need to have a sense of what it will cost you to start and maintain your business, as well as paying your personal expenses, and how to plan for that. One of my clients quit her day job, but didn't plan for how she would pay her bills while she built her business. She ended up having to take an interim part-time job to cover her expenses while she built her clientele, which she did eventually. (See more about a Transition Plan on page 65.)

How will you finance your business? Some businesses need very little start-up capital, others a lot. Some common ways of financing a new practice include:

- Your own savings
- Loans from banks (possibly an SBA [Small Business Association] loan), credit unions or credit cards
- Partners
- Investors – these could be family or friends, not necessarily venture capitalists

Take the time to write out some Income and Expense projections, so that you can be prepared when you're ready to make the leap. If spreadsheets make your eyes glaze over, get help from a friend or accountant. It doesn't have to be difficult or complicated.

Use the worksheets on the following pages to create your business plan and income projections. An example of a financial spreadsheet is provided to get you started.

To make it a little more fun, try Jennifer Lee's *The Right-Brain Business Plan*.

Business Plan Checklist

Preparation
- Education, training
- Degrees, licensing, certifications

Business form
- Sole proprietorship
- Partnership
- Corporation: S-Corp or LLC

Visioning
- Business name and professional title
- Mission/vision statements
- Goals for the business

Branding
- Niche or focus
- Target audience
- Unique selling point (USP)
- Services and products
- Pricing

Employees and supporting services
- Lawyer
- Accountant
- Bookkeeper
- Assistant or virtual assistant
- Web designer/manager
- Editor/proofreader
- Sub-contractors:

_____

_____

_____

Operations
- Office or workspace
  - Furnishings
  - Technology
  - Forms of communication (phone, email, post office box, etc.)
- Client materials
- Promotional materials: business cards, letterhead, postcards, flyers, brochures, etc.
- Online promotion: website, social media, listings on related websites, etc.
- Recordkeeping
- Taxes
- Insurance
- Bank account
- Accepting payments: credit cards, money transfers

Planning for Success
- Financial Plan
- Transition Plan
- Marketing Plan

Financial Projections

	Month 1	Month 2	Month 3
PROJECTED INCOME			
Services			
Products			
Other income			
Total Income			
START-UP COSTS			
Office security deposit			
Equipment (computer, printer, professional tools)			
Furniture			
Printed materials (business cards, brochures, stationery)			
Website (domain, hosting, design)			
Incorporation fees			
ONGOING EXPENSES			
Rent or mortgage – home			
Rent – office			
Utilities			
Salaries or contractor payments			
Payroll taxes			
Phone(s) (land line, cell)			
Internet, wi-fi, website maintenance			
Other services (Zoom, data protection, etc.)			
Advertising and promotion			
Insurance (liability, property, health)			
Loan payments			
Federal estimated taxes			
State estimated taxes			
Equipment (purchases, maintenance, insurance)			
Legal and accounting fees			
Office supplies and postage			
Professional memberships and meetings			
Continuing education			
Publications (books, magazines, journals)			
Credit card and bank fees			
Business travel / car expenses			
Clothing			
Food			
Other personal expenses (entertainment, gas, travel, etc.)			
Miscellaneous expenses			
Total Expenses (Start-Up + Ongoing)			

Transition Plan

Before you leap into the void, think about a transition plan – how you will get from where you are now to launching and having a profitable practice. This may include:

- Learning new skills and practicing them
- Getting any required degrees, certifications or licenses
- Moonlighting or starting a business on the side, while you keep your "day job"
- Making inroads into a new industry by joining an association and networking with colleagues in that field
- Building up your cash reserves, so you can pay your bills until your business becomes profitable
- Setting up your business infrastructure, including legal and financial needs, recordkeeping, and office or workspace
- Working with your family to agree upon and prepare for any changes in lifestyle

When you're making a career change, you usually start by obtaining the necessary training, skills and knowledge. You may also need to qualify for certification or licensing. In some professions, such as coaching or massage, new practitioners often begin by working with pro bono or "practice" clients, serving under an experienced professional or starting a small practice on the side to build their skill and confidence. As you become established, you may need, or want, continuing education courses, as well as books, trade publications and online tutorials to hone and sharpen your skills or to maintain your credentials.

Get a foothold in your new field by joining your professional association and networking with your new colleagues, either in person or virtually. Having these contacts also helps you strengthen your new identity as a professional in this business. It's also helpful to connect with more experienced colleagues who might serve as mentors or advisors, as well as others like yourself who are just starting out. These connections can turn into strategic alliances down the line – either partners who you can join forces with to do workshops or presentations, to refer clients to colleagues with different specialties or to meet compatible colleagues in the same or various professions to form a "mastermind group"*. If you have a great rapport and complementary skill sets, you might even go into business together.

---

*A group of trusted professionals who meet on a regular schedule (often monthly) to support each other with business issues and practice-building. From a concept developed by Napoleon Hill.

If your profession has publications or websites, consider subscribing to stay on top of industry news and gain useful tips.

If you're leaving a job to start your own business using your established skill set and you're bringing some clients with you, you may be able to leap right into a profitable business. If you're starting from scratch, seriously consider maintaining another source of income while you build your new practice, and phase that out slowly. It's hard to project confidence to prospective clients when you're exuding desperation about paying your bills. As your practice builds, you might go from a full-time to a part-time job, and eventually phase that out as well – although some propreneurs enjoy having a variety of income streams from different jobs or professions that they enjoy.

Either way, it's important to have a financial cushion. You may need it to cover your expenses during the start-up phase, until your business becomes profitable or as a back-up for slow periods or emergencies. If you have transition money in the bank, it gives you the freedom to quit your full-time job and focus on building your new business without having to devote forty or more hours a week to another job. Just as with a salaried job, aim to have six to nine months of living expenses in savings. It's not an absolute must, but it sure gives you peace of mind as business ebbs and flows.

It's also helpful to learn to manage cash flow. It's tempting to indulge yourself when there's a lot of money coming in, but it can be scary during slow periods, when you're not sure you can cover your basic expenses or have to dip into savings. As you go through your first year or two of business, keep a spreadsheet of income and expenses by month (see sample on page 64), so you get a sense of what to expect in terms of cash flow and can plan for future years. Hopefully, your receivables will increase, so that you have a little more disposable income to enjoy. You may have to make some sacrifices at first, but with a little hard work and preparation, you'll have more freedom as your business grows.

In setting up your business, think about the various items listed in the Operations section (see page 56). Some businesses have a fairly low start-up cost — perhaps some office furniture, computer, phone, and a bookshelf or filing cabinet. Others need a work space and specialized equipment. You'll also need to invest time and money in some form of advertising or marketing to connect with potential clients. You may also need to engage a lawyer or CPA to establish your business as a legal entity, as well as handling taxes.

"Survival Jobs" and Multiple Streams of Income

When I was an actress, it was common to have "survival jobs" to pay your bills between acting jobs. There was no shame in it; it was just part of the business.

Many new practitioners start with a side business while they're working a full-time job. When you know you have at least a base income, you can relax and be more authentic in your sales and marketing process. As your business builds, you can reduce your hours and eventually quit entirely, if that's what you want. You may have another profession that you enjoy, or you may just like the security of having some steady income as your practice ebbs and flows. So, you may continue working part-time or have another side business doing something else that you also enjoy, such as making and selling jewelry or teaching yoga. Go with what feels good to you and makes you feel financially safe and personally fulfilled.

Time Management

As you're launching your new business, there's a good possibility that you're continuing to work full-time, taking classes to enhance your skills, and perhaps have a family and other responsibilities and activities. Your schedule may be packed and you may be exhausted. But you have to find time if you want to get your practice off the ground.

Create a plan. Start slowly. It may take more time than you'd like, especially if you're in a job you're desperate to get out of, but you need to be realistic about what you can do without burning yourself out or risking your financial or physical well-being. It's also hard to perform well in your work when you're frazzled and exhausted.

Set aside a few hours a week to work on your business plan, set up your work space, create client materials and record-keeping, abd work on marketing – however much time you can realistically afford.

As you put your business infrastructure in place, continue to practice with some clients (paid or pro bono, if applicable) to keep your skills in shape as you grow your business. You may set aside one evening a week or half a day on the weekend to work with clients. If it takes you months, or even years, before you can fully get your practice off the ground, you don't want to get out of practice and have to start all over. It's also easier to sell yourself to new clients when you're actually plying your trade and you feel confident about your work.

Tip: Bolster your confidence by keeping a list of client successes that you can refer to when doubts creep in. Read it before you meet with a client or speak to a potential client.

One of the biggest challenges for new practitioners is marketing their services. We'll look at that next.

But first, use the worksheet on the following page to plan your transition.

My Transition/Time Management Plan

		Time Line

- Learn new skills
- Acquire certification, degree or license

Example: Complete certification program	March – September 2024

- Create a budget and financial projections
- Create a financial buffer

Example: put aside 10% of my take-home pay	Now through December 2024

- Rent space or set up a home office
- Purchase furniture and equipment
- Build my website

- Meet with clients

Example:	Tuesdays and Thursdays, 6 – 8 pm

- Cut job to part-time, increase my practice

Example:	Go to part-time by January 2025
	Network one night a week
	Meet with clients Tuesdays and Thursdays
		from 10 am – 8 pm with meal breaks

- Quit my day job, practice full-time

Example:	By September 2025
	Meet with clients 4 days a week from
		10 am to 8 pm with meal breaks

- Additional sources of income:

Chapter 5: Marketing Your New Business

In order to have a thriving business, you have to reach out and connect with potential clients who would benefit from your services or products. Some people enjoy this and others dread this part of running a business.

Marketing and sales can be a challenge for the propreneur. For one thing, you may be great at what you do, but know nothing about marketing. Or you may feel uncomfortable promoting yourself. The bad news is, marketing is necessary if you want to have clients. The good news is, there are many ways to market, and you can choose methods that are most comfortable and appealing to you. You may even grow to enjoy it more than you expected.

Marketing is a huge topic in itself, so I'm just going to cover a few key points here. For more information, there are tons of websites, marketing specialists and books, many of which are geared toward specific professions. My book, *Creative Marketing Tools for Coaches*, has useful tips for life coaches and anyone in private practice.

Marketing by Doing What You Love

There are a lot of marketing "tips" out there that claim that you need to spend half your day on social media in order to get clients. First of all, it's not true. There are many ways to connect with your target audience. And if you set yourself up with marketing tools that you hate, you're going to avoid it as much as you can – not helpful when you need to get clients.

The philosophy that I've found most effective is to market doing what you love, using your natural gifts and talents. When you do that, you connect with people more authentically, and you don't have to feel you're out there "hawking your wares," an approach that many propreneurs abhor. By sharing what you do from the heart, people are more likely to connect with you, especially in professions like coaching and healing, where having a personal connection is crucial. Even if you hire a copywriter to write for your website and promotional materials, start by writing it yourself to make sure it authentically reflects you and doesn't sound like "marketing copy."

> "If you're not willing to show up as you, your clients can never find you."
>
> ~ Michael Neill

Some examples of ways to market naturally:

- If you're a people person, get out and rub elbows with your target audience or good referral sources (other professionals who work with the same types of people as you do), or actively participate on relevant social networking sites.
- If you enjoy public speaking or teaching, find places to do presentations, workshops and seminars. Many people are scared of public speaking, but if you feel motivated to do this, start small and build your competence and confidence.
- Along with public speaking, you can do podcasts and post videos on YouTube and your own website.
- If you're a web designer, create a great website for yourself that demonstrates both the creative and technical aspects of your craft.
- As a graphic designer, you can design beautiful brochures, flyers, business cards and ads.
- If you're a good writer, do a blog, newsletter, e-booklets and even books. A newsletter is a great way to build a database, where you can communicate directly with your followers to let them know about a new blog, a special offer, a webinar, etc.

With a plethora of online publishing resources, anyone can self-publish their book fairly economically. (I do recommend utilizing professional editors and designers to produce a quality product.) If you're looking for a broader audience – for example, if you want to develop a reputation as a motivational speaker – you might go the traditional route and find an agent who can represent you to major publishing houses. My book, *Creative Marketing Tools for Coaches*, goes into this in greater detail, and there are many other resources available if you choose to seek out a publisher.

Setting the Foundation: Website and Social Media

Back in the "olden days," when you started a business, you would get a listing in the Yellow Pages and take out ads in relevant publications. The twenty-first-century equivalent is having a website and a social media presence.

Website

In most cases, a website will be a must (especially if you're a website designer!). People search for services on the web, and having a professional website gives you visibility and credibility. You don't have to have an extensive website to get started; you can begin with a few pages that clearly represent what you do and how to contact you. There are numerous do-it-yourself web hosts with reasonable fees and attractive templates.

As discussed previously, make sure that your desired domain is available before you lock in your business name. (See page 51.)

Before you create your website, think about what you want people to experience. You want a website that represents you properly. How do you want people to feel when they view your website? What colors, words or pictures will give visitors to your website that experience? I've worked with new coaches who use words like "optimistic," "joyful," "enthusiastic" and "inspired," and then create websites that are dark and weighty.

If you're on a budget, use an inexpensive service such as Fiverr or find a design student looking to build their portfolio to get a custom-designed logo, and use royalty-free clip art that represents your type of practice and clients. Stay away from generic landscapes and sunsets – unless that's what you're selling! Choose graphics that more specifically represent your business, or work with an illustrator or photographer to create unique custom images.

Social Media

As we know, social media can be a "black hole" that sucks up your time and energy. Even if you love it, prioritize how much time you'll spend each day, which social media sites best connect with your target audience and which ones you enjoy. Some of the most popular ones as of this writing are Facebook, Instagram and LinkedIn, among many others.

Similar to websites, many people search for services on social media, so it is important to have at least a basic presence and post something periodically to keep your audience engaged. People may not contact you immediately for your services, but the more they get to know you, the more you'll be top of mind when the need arises.

Budget productive time on social media. Plan what you'll post and how often. Stimulate discussion by asking questions or inviting people to comment. Join discussion groups and participate actively. It may be scary to be visible in the wider community, but remember, you don't have to reveal information that's too personal. If you're new to a particular platform, explore it, see what others are posting and what's effective in connecting with potential clients. Then jump in, experiment, fine tune as you go along and get help if you need it.

Other Ways to Market

There are numerous other ways to market, both online and in person.

- **Get listings on referral sites**

    Many professional associations and trade publications, such as *Psychology Today* and the International Coaching Federation, offer a referral service. This may be included as part of a membership or a separate paid service. There are also general business listings, such as Yelp.

Use your judgment on paying for listings. Since coaching has been so popular, there are many referral listings where you can pay a hefty fee, and then get lost in the crowd and not get any referrals. If you can get a free listing on a relevant site, it doesn't hurt to take it. All links back to your website help with search engine optimization (SEO).

- **Network and connect with referral sources**

    Look for other practitioners or businesses that complement yours and work with the same or similar clientele. See if they're willing to refer potential clients to you and, if appropriate, refer clients to them. Some examples:

    - Accountants and bookkeepers: attend small business meetings and conferences, peruse published listings of new businesses
    - Virtual assistants: search for listings of professionals who need administrative help, register on service websites such as Upwork, Guru and VA-specific listing sites
    - Massage therapists: connect with health clubs and spas, hotel concierges and other health and wellness professionals
    - Life, career and executive coaches: attend business networking meetings, contact therapists and counselors, health practitioners, human resource departments and Employee Assistance Programs (EAP)
    - Web and graphic designers: contact small business accountants and bookkeepers, join chambers of commerce, get listed and respond to project proposals on referral services such as Guru or Upwork

- **Offer workshops and presentations**

    These are a great way to connect with potential clients, because you meet them face-to-face, either in person or on videoconference. Zoom classes are easy and cost-effective and can be promoted globally on social media.

    Some places to present locally include: libraries, wellness centers, colleges, adult learning centers, community centers, etc. You can either work with an organization that has a catalog (i.e., does some of the marketing for you) and provides workshop space, or rent space and advertise on your own.

The bottom line: Don't be intimidated by marketing. There are tons of resources and people you can hire, and you can always learn some new tricks. Take it a step at a time, see what works, eliminate what doesn't and build from there. You'll develop some new skills and, hopefully, come to enjoy it!

Section III: Operating Your Business

Once your business is up and running, you can relax into it and enjoy it, but you don't want to become complacent and feel you can coast forever. Clients come and go, the market changes, and you have to keep up or risk having your business go under for lack of attention.

The Daily "Grind" and Work/Life Balance

Hopefully, you'll love your business so much that it won't be a grind!

As the boss, and especially if you're a one-person business, you have to pay attention to your operations on a daily basis. If your client roster is dwindling, you'll need to get out and "pound the pavement." You'll need to keep an eye on your income and expenses to make sure that your business remains profitable and covers your expenses, along with paying yourself and saving for emergencies and retirement.

You'll also need to manage your work/life balance, especially if you're working from home, where the boundaries can easily get blurred. You want to put the time and effort into your business, but you also need to make sure you're taking care of yourself: eating healthy; getting exercise; getting enough sleep; taking time off (regular days off and vacations); and having time for family, friends and fun. You may feel like you can't afford to take time for these things, but believe me, if you don't take care of yourself, your business will suffer.

Serving Your Customers/Managing Products and Services

The most important part of your business is, of course, serving your clientele. Hopefully, you're spending most of your time doing this, and both you and your clients are happy and satisfied.

As your business grows, you may need to hire extra help. You may already have an assistant, a bookkeeper and someone to manage your website and social media. If not, see what help you can hire that will free you up to focus on the money-making activities.

As you build your business, keep your eye on the marketplace to see what you need to do to remain competitive. This may mean developing new products or services that your client base wants. It's also a great way to keep yourself fresh, so you're not just doing the same thing repetitively and getting bored.

You might ask your clients for feedback or set up a survey on SurveyMonkey or your social media to get ideas for new products and services. If you're networking with your colleagues and reading trade publications, those will also give you ideas.

If it's appropriate for your type of business, you might want to develop products that provide a stream of passive income. For example, you might develop books, e-books, audios, videos, self-study programs or product lines that enhance your business. Many health practitioners sell supplements or items that complement their work, such as yoga mats, t-shirts, cosmetics and other self-care products. Designers may sell journals, notecards, calendars, t-shirts, tote bags and mugs that feature their art or photographs. (Check out Café Press and Zazzle for ideas.)

As your business grows, think about what you can do to grow your income with less effort. Developing new products and services can also be fun and creatively stimulating. You may want to subcontract with others in your profession to serve more clients and expand your reach. This may be someone who does the less-skilled parts of your work or a peer, perhaps someone with a different specialty, who's happy to get client referrals from you for a commission.

Client Records

If you have recurring clients, you'll want to keep a record of their work with you. It'll be handy to refer back to this for continuity. As a health practitioner, you may want to keep track of how your treatments are helping, or not. As a life coach, you'll want to track your clients' progress and keep notes on additional goals or issues that your clients might want to work on. If you're doing some sort of design, it's a good idea to archive your digital documents, so you don't have to recreate a project from scratch if the client wants updates.

In some professions, you'll be required to do reporting on your clients. Even if it's for yourself, it's good to keep track of how you've worked with your clients, as well as payment records (see the next section). You'll be able to serve your clients more effectively and, in the case that something goes wrong, you'll have a "paper" trail.

Managing Finances

We talked in chapter 4 about setting up your finances. They need to be managed on an ongoing basis. Setting them up correctly from the beginning will make that easier.

If your business is a sole proprietorship, an S-Corp or an LLC, your personal and business finances may be somewhat comingled. Meet with your accountant to determine the best way to provide tax information to them to make the process easier for both of you.

If you're an old-fashioned type of person, set up a paper spreadsheet or an Excel file. For accounting software, Quicken is easy and popular. Quickbooks will give you additional functions, such as inventory and invoicing. Both can create and print reports. Ask your accountant, bookkeeper or colleagues what they recommend and how to set up categories. Choose whatever method is easiest for you, so that you keep it up on a regular basis. I've made a habit of logging in income and expenses every Sunday. When tax time comes, I simply print out reports from Quicken and drop the numbers into an Excel spreadsheet that I reuse every year, which has the categories set up the way my accountant likes them.

Keep records of all income

If you're working with private clients, they will most likely be paying you by credit card, money transfers or occasionally by check or cash. Log all receipts into your bookkeeping software.

I do recommend claiming all income, even if it's given to you in cash. For one thing, it establishes you as a professional and honors professional ethics. It also allows you to claim business expenses up to the amount of income you earn from that business. And thinking long-term, the higher your income, the higher your Social Security payments will be when you're ready to retire.

If you need to document your income, your credit card provider (e.g., Square or Paypal) should allow you to print out sales reports; you can also save the receipt for each transaction. Make copies of checks or, if you use mobile deposits, keep the checks. Print out records of money transfers. For cash receipts, well, just record them.

Keep receipts for business expenses

Log all your business expenses into your spreadsheet or software. Quicken and Quickbooks allow you to set up categories, so that you can easily create a report to see what your expenses were in each category for tax purposes, as well as keeping an eye on your expenditures and profit margins.

Again, I recommend entering these expenses on a regular basis. When I get a credit card bill, I log in each expense and assign a category. It's laborious, but it saves a lot of time and stress at tax time.

You may have heard of the proverbial shoe box where people keep their receipts. You do need to keep the receipts as backup (preferably organized by category), but if you log them into your software, you won't have to dread tax season quite so much or pay extra to your accountant to organize it for you.

Common business expenses include:

- Office space (outside or home office)
- Office supplies and equipment
- Computer hardware, software, repair, supplies
- Business travel or local transportation if you use your car for business
- Phone (landline, cell phone)
- Internet/wi-fi
- Advertising (website, social media ads, printed materials and other paid advertising)
- Education (classes, books, audios, videos, etc.)
- Business meetings
- Professional memberships
- Insurance
- Credit card fees
- Bank fees

Manage cash flow

Since your income and expenses will vary from month to month, keep an eye on your cash flow. You can have your bookkeeper or accountant monitor this for you, but keep in mind that this will incur additional fees for their services.

If you do this yourself, sit down with your accountant and set up a system for managing your cash flow. Make sure you're paying your personal and business expenses and putting some aside as a cushion. As with any profession, work toward having a three- to six-month emergency fund and putting money into retirement investments. Aside from your accountant, you may work with a certified financial planner to see what strategy and financial products work best for you. Even if you're still young, don't neglect this. The earlier you start – even if you start with only a small amount per month – the more you'll have for a comfortable retirement. Your future self will be grateful!

Pay estimated taxes

Work with your accountant to figure out how much to pay each quarter and DON'T FORGET TO PAY THIS QUARTERLY to avoid penalties you can incur if you wait until you file your taxes the following year.

In the beginning, you might pay 15% of your receipts for the quarter for federal estimated and 10% for state (unless your state doesn't have income tax). Once your income stabilizes, your accountant can divide the annual amount into four quarterly payments and provide you with preprinted forms to submit. If you're able to pay online, use those as a guideline for how much to pay.

Sales tax

If you're selling products, be sure to charge the appropriate sales tax for all sales within your state. The rate can vary by county, so consult the tax charts for your state. If your sales are high, file sales tax quarterly. If not, filing annually will be sufficient.

Remember that if you're purchasing products for resale, you can provide your vendor with a resale certificate, so that they don't have to charge you sales tax.

See page 55 for more on sales tax.

File taxes annually

Depending on whether you're functioning as a sole proprietor or a corporation (S-Corp or LLC), you'll file your personal taxes and claim expenses on Schedule C, or you'll need to file a separate set of corporate taxes.

You're probably used to filing your taxes by April 15. Corporate taxes are due by March 15, so you'll have to hustle to get them done sooner. Since personal and corporate work together, just get them done together and it'll all be done by March 15! If you've kept up your recordkeeping throughout the year, this should be doable.

And More Marketing ...

Marketing is something you need to keep doing, even when your business is up and running. You may have a full client roster, but people move on and you'll need to fill those empty spots.

You need to keep potential customers "in the pipeline" by actively marketing on a continual basis. Financial planners network to bring in new clients. Many health practitioners do educational presentations. Writing articles or blogs and doing Facebook or Instagram Lives or YouTube videos are great ways to stay in front of potential customers. You might offer a referral fee or a free session to encourage your current clients or referral sources to spread the word about your services.

Hopefully by now, you've got your marketing infrastructure in place: website, social media, email database and any other marketing tools that are effective in connecting with your customer base. You've gotten some momentum and you're spending more time serving your clients than looking for new ones.

In some cases, where personal connection is important, you'll need to do these marketing activities yourself. Now that you've got an income stream, you might hire a marketing or social media professional or virtual assistant to take some of it off your plate, so you can focus on working with clients and making money. Even then, you want to have a presence in your marketing outlets. Potential clients want to connect with you as well as your products and services.

You may be concerned about attracting more customers than you can handle. You can certainly pace your marketing accordingly. I get solicitations from marketers to generate 50 leads a week for me. As a solo practitioner, it would be absurd to pursue that. But a couple of inquiries a week is manageable.

If necessary, you can put eager customers on a waiting list or backorder products. If it's really more than you can handle, have a list of compatible colleagues who you can refer to. If it happens a lot, you might negotiate a referral fee or subcontract with one or more practitioners in your field to take on the overflow for a commission.

As mentioned earlier, there are tons of resources for marketing. Many are industry-specific, such as marketing books for life coaches. Some of them are what I call "high octane." These are great if you're energetic and highly motivated. If you're more of a Tortoise, find resources that fit your style and work for your type of practice, and then keep working with them regularly. Slow and steady wins the race!

Section IV: Pulling It All Together

Now that you've got all the steps, a few final words …

Determination and Commitment

It drives me crazy when I coach someone to come up with a new life or career path and they say, "Yeah, well, I hope it happens." Well, yeah, there are no guarantees, but don't you think you're more likely to succeed when you're determined and committed? Think of it as a speed bump. Are you more likely to get over the bump if you amble along tentatively at 20 mph or if you floor it?

> "What this power is, I cannot say. All I know is that it exists …
> and it becomes available only when you are in that state of mind in which you know exactly what you want … and are fully determined not to quit until you get it."
> ~ Alexander Graham Bell

When I started my coaching business, I went through a two-year period where I had let go of my "survival" job and was putting 100% of my time and energy into my business – working with clients, marketing, designing and giving workshops, and going to networking events while I had the time. During those two years, I made very little money and fell back on my savings. Sure, it was a scary time, but after two years, I had a roster of clients, and two big teaching opportunities came my way that put my business on solid ground. From then on, I was able to make a living doing what I love. If I had quit after a year, I would have ended up back in a job that paid the bills, but was not meaningful for me.

Get Support

Remember, even if you're a solopreneur, you don't have to do it alone. Get emotional and practical support from friends and family (not the naysayers!). Make professional connections. Join a business incubator or put together a mastermind group with trusted colleagues. Hire professionals to help you with the parts that are challenging for you, so you can focus your time on the money-making activities that you do well and enjoy.

While failure may feel shameful, don't hide your fears and mistakes. If you do, it's more likely that those mistakes will sink your business. Take classes to enhance your skill set. Hire consultants and coaches who can guide you and get you through the rough spots, so that your business can thrive. Own your mistakes, and course-correct as needed.

Stay Focused and Motivated

No matter how much you love your business, there will be times when you feel overwhelmed and discouraged. As your own boss, you won't have someone standing over you to get things done. You have to manage yourself.

Here are a few tips to help you stay focused and motivated.

- **Be accountable to someone else**

    Many of us have no problem breaking commitments to ourself, but if we've declared an intention to someone else, it becomes embarrassing to not follow through. Have a coach, colleague or mastermind group, or even a friend, who will hold you to your promises.

- **Make appointments or commitments to others**

    Similarly, if you make an appointment to meet someone or schedule a presentation, it will force you to show up. Many people don't take self-imposed deadlines seriously, but they will meet a deadline if it involves keeping a commitment to someone else.

    One of my clients scheduled breakfast meetings to get himself up and out. Once he got going, he would continue working on his business during the day. If you want to do workshops, get one scheduled a reasonable amount of time in the future, and then get to work on it. Having your presentation advertised and showing up unprepared will be embarrassing, so you're more likely to push through the resistance and get it done.

- **Make it a priority**

    In *The War of Art*, Stephen Pressfield talks about treating your creative work as a business, and not as a hobby. You don't have to go so far out on a limb that you frighten yourself (more than necessary – a little fear comes with the territory), but schedule time to work on your business on a regular basis and make that time sacred.

- **Stay excited about the business**

    Even if you love what you do, it may eventually become routine or even boring. Find ways that you can bring your creativity into play and breathe new energy into your business with new products and services.

- **Be prepared to deal with tough times and parts you don't enjoy**

    Even a business you love won't always be fun and easy. Things won't always run smoothly. You'll make mistakes. Life will throw you curve balls. Be prepared, so that you're not functioning on the edge where one mistake will be impossible to recover from.

If something happens, first of all, don't beat yourself up. If you made a mistake, do what you can to recover and assess what you could do better next time. There's always a learning curve, and mistakes will help you to run your business in a better way going forward.

Have a financial cushion, so that if you make a costly mistake, it won't sink your business and put you in debt.

Be willing to see things from a different perspective and redirect as needed. Change can be challenging, but it will also bring new energy to your business.

If possible, delegate or outsource what you can of what you don't enjoy or that you're not good at. Hopefully, as your business becomes more profitable, you'll have greater means to hire others to do the parts that are drudgery for you or that don't tap into your strengths.

- **Build in rewards**

    Even if you love your work, you can't be focusing on it 24/7. You may be scared that if you don't devote all of your available time to it, it will fall apart. But burning yourself out is a sure road to failure, and it won't do much for your health.

    If this is your livelihood, make sure you can pay yourself a living wage, or hang onto an outside job until you can do that. Take care of yourself, so you don't burn out. Put boundaries around your work day and work week. Take days off and make sure to build in vacation time. Your clientele will be happy to work around your schedule, or you can hire someone or get a colleague to cover for you while you're off recharging.

The Tortoise Way: Patience and Persistence

Launching and growing a new business can take time. As a Tortoise, your energy may be limited or you may be a slow mover. Chances are, you'll feel overwhelmed and discouraged at some point. Don't quit. Stay committed for the long haul. Do your best to have a solid financial cushion, so that you can securely pay your bills while you're building your business.

Remember, slow and steady wins the race. Be patient and persistent. Don't let up. Keep the momentum going. Sure, there may come a time when it's clear the business is not taking off, and you may need to come up with a new plan. But don't go into it with your eye on the exit door. It takes courage, but you don't want to quit five minutes before the miracle occurs!

Finally, operate your business in a way that creates a lifestyle that you enjoy. Isn't that the point? To do what you love and live a life that feels good. What could be better than that?!

Resources*

Books and Audios

- *Creative Marketing Tools for Coaches,* by Sharon Good
- *The Tortoise Workbook: Strategies for Getting Ahead at Your Own Pace,* by Sharon Good
- *Secrets of Self-Employment: Surviving and Thriving on the Ups and Downs of Being Your Own Boss,* by Sarah and Paul Edwards
- *Business Partnership Essentials: A Step-by-Step Action Plan for Succeeding in Business With a Partner*, by Dorene Lehavi, PhD
- *You, Inc.: The Art of Selling Yourself*, by Harry Beckwith and Christine K. Clifford

Business Plan and Development

- *The Right-Brain Business Plan: A Creative, Visual Map for Success*, by Jennifer Lee
- Live Plan business plan software – www.liveplan.com
- Small Business Association – www.sba.gov – Business Guide > Plan Your Business > Write Your Business Plan
- SCORE – www.score.org
- Entrepreneur – www.entrepreneur.com – Search "business plan"

Practice Management

- Coaches Console – https://coachesconsole.com
- Honeybook – www.honeybook.com
- Dubsado – www.dubsado.com
- Satori – https://satoriapp.com
- Paperbell – https://paperbell.com/
- CoachAccountable – www.coachaccountable.com/
- Acuity Scheduling – www.acuityscheduling.com
- Calendly scheduling – https://calendly.com/
- Search "practice management for [your business]"

*Disclaimer: All resources are offered as suggestions. Be sure to check them out for yourself.

Writing Proposals

- *Persuasive Business Proposals*, by Tom Sant
- *Million Dollar Consulting Proposals*, by Alan Weiss
- *Proposal Best Practices*, by David Seibert

Accepting Payments

- Paypal.com
- Squareup.com
- Stripe.com
- Venmo.com
- Zelle – www.zellepay.com or your bank

See also Practice Management resources

Writing, Editing and Design Services

- Upwork.com
- Guru.com
- Fiverr.com

Virtual Assistants

- AssistU – https://www.workwithava.com/
- Search "virtual assistants"

Mission Statements

- MissionStatements.com
- Use the Mission Statement Builder under the Resources tab at FranklinCovey.com

Inspiration

- *Callings: Finding and Following an Authentic Life*, by Gregg Levoy
- *What Should I Do With My Life?* by Po Bronson
- *Working Identity: Unconventional Strategies for Reinventing Your Career*, by Herminia Ibarra

About the Author

Sharon Good, a self-proclaimed Tortoise, is President of Good Life Coaching Inc. and a Life, Career, Retirement and Creativity Coach based in New York City. With a rich variety of personal and professional experiences informing her work, she coaches artists to achieve their creative and professional goals and helps individuals from all walks of life create fulfilling lives, unique career paths and enriching retirements.

She has trained life and career coaches for the Life Purpose Institute, the Creativity Coaching Association and NYU's School of Professional Studies, as well as offering personal and professional enrichment workshops for the 92nd Street Y and numerous other venues in the New York City area and through teleclasses and webinars.

Sharon is the author of several books published by Excalibur Publishing, Sourcebooks and, currently, Good Life Press. These include *Creative Marketing Tools for Coaches: Use Your Natural Gifts to Attract Your Ideal Clients*, *The Tortoise Workbook: Strategies for Getting Ahead at Your Own Pace*, *Managing With A Heart: 222 Ways to Make Your Employees Feel Appreciated* and *Powerful Choices, Powerful Life*.

A graduate of Hofstra University, she is certified in Life and Career Coaching by the Life Purpose Institute, Retirement Coaching by Retirement Options, and holds a certificate in Adult Career Planning and Development from New York University. She has held certifications from the International Coaching Federation and the Center for Credentialing and Education.

Sharon's websites:
www.goodlifecoaching.com
www.goodlifepress.com

www.ingramcontent.com/pod-product-compliance
Lightning Source LLC
Chambersburg PA
CBHW061821290426
44110CB00027B/2938